The Siren's Guitar

The Siren's Guitar

A Musical Paddling Adventure

Stephen Snyder

Felton, California

The Siren's Guitar: A Musical Paddling Adventure
Copyright © 2011 by Stephen Snyder

All rights reserved. No part of this book may be reproduced, stored in a retrieval system, or transmitted, in any form or by any means, electronic, mechanical, photocopying, recording, or otherwise, without the written prior permission of the author, except in the case of brief quotations embodied in critical articles and reviews.

Cover Design by Jessica Moreno

All photographs were taken by the author and Justin Burrows
Siren woodcut design by Hannah Nevins
Cover Photograph by Chris Bratt www.chrisbratt.com

ISBN 978-1-935914-11-2

Printed in the United States of America

Additional copies available from:

www.spiritualpathfinder.com

RIVER SANCTUARY PUBLISHING
P.O Box 1561
Felton, CA 95018
www.riversanctuarypublishing.com
Dedicated to the awakening of the New Earth

To Liam and Sonia: My Magical Ones

Acknowledgments

I would like to thank: John Schechter for introducing me to the siren story, and Thomas Turino for inspiring writing. My friends, Wendy Thompson and Lisa Marrack, for their comments and corrections on early drafts of the book and much needed grammatical help. Margaret and Mark from Kayak Connection and Marc Allen from New Wold library for giving encouragement on early versions of the book. Blessings to Annie and David from River Sanctuary Publishing who have been absolutely wonderful to collaborate with, and have helped me to realize a dream of having a book on the bookshelf. To my Bolivian connections, in particular "Cookie" Audas and her cousin Bernie - un gran abrazo. A huge thank you to my wonderful artist friends Hannah Nevins and Chris Bratt for creating the sirena picture, and the photograph she lies in. Thank you to Kevin DiNoto who spent many an hour in coffee shops with me as I worked on this book. Over the years I have had two wonderful sound engineers, Pete Coates and John Reynolds, who I want to thank for capturing the sound of my charango so beautifully in the recording studio and out in the field. A special heartfelt thanks to Justin Burrows who took this adventure with me, and helped me to create a truly wonderful and unforgettable experience. A special obrigada to my Brazilian mom who instilled the capacity for believing in the unexplainable happenings (orbs!!) in the world. And of course all my love to my wonderful partner in the water world, Gwynne.

ISLANDS OF LAKE TITICACA
(painting)

Isla del Sol

Copacabana Peninsula

Isla de la Luna

The Siren's Guitar

Preface 1

It All Started...
    1-Charangos 7
    2-The Andean *Sirena* 10
    3-My Travel Partner 13

In Search of the Perfect Charango
    1-Arriving 17
    2-La Paz 19
    3-Charango Day 21
    4-The Perfect Charango 23
    5-Altitude Sickness 26

Copacabana
    1-Heading Off 31
    2-The Bus Ride 33
    3-Copacabana Memories 37
    4-Copacabana *Otra Vez* 39
    5-Trip Philosophy 42
    6-Trout – We Want Them! 44
    7-Treasure Hunting 46
    8-The Last Meal 48

Lake Titicaca
    1-Finally on the Water 53
    2-Out on the Lake 56
    3-Rugged Coastline 59
    4-First Camp 62
    5-Sirenando 68
    6-Cold Night 73
    7-First Morning 75
    8-The Man 79
    9-Passing Through History 83
    10-Yampupata 84

Isla del Sol

1–Isla del Sol Arrival 89
2–Tides? 91
3–Yumani 93
4–The Song Revealed 101
5–Unsettling Caves 106
6–Sacred Rocks 110
7–Proper Forms of Sirenando 117
8–Phone Home 120
9–Mysterious Islands 122
10–The Beach 126
11–Soaking It In 133
12–Uakti 135
13–Yumani, Take Two 138
14–The Gringo Road 141

Isla de la Luna

1–Isla de la Luna 149
2–Pachamama Festival 152
3–The Ceremony 154
4–Walking Around Isla de la Luna 157
5–Iñak Uyu – Court of Women 160

The Journey Home

1–Back to the Mainland 165
2–Return to Copacabana 168
3–Strange Water 170
4–Last Night in the Copa 172
5–Bus Ride home and Almost Killing Someone 174
   The Siren's Call 176

City Sirenas

1–Looking for a Siren Song in the City 179
2–Airport Adventure 186

The Song On and On

1–Taking the Siren Song Home 193
2–Taking the Sirena to Work 195

Preface

I woke up every half hour to check my watch, and finally at about 4:45, was ready to get my clothes on and check my instrument. Still dark outside, I grabbed my headlamp, but kept it turned off and headed for the cave. There it was...my charango, shining in the starry night. Beautiful. I picked it up, strummed it...and it sounded different. Noticeably different, and my heart raced.

    This is a true story about attempting to hear a siren's song along the coast of two islands, Isla del Sol (Island of the Sun) and Isla de la Luna (Island of the Moon) in Lake Titicaca, where such musical experiences have been reputed to occur. The emphasis of this adventure is on the musical experience and not on the poor siren, who has been searched for, chased, pleaded with and sullied by the imagination of the lovelorn for thousands of years. I do not wish to follow the fate of these bewitched souls, smashed up on the rocky shores with broken a heart. I am not in search of an other-worldly affair with a half woman, half fish. I am happily married to a wonderful woman, thank you. I am just interested in the possibility, no matter how improbable, of actually hearing a siren's song. I have always been fascinated by the origins of song and melody and the siren's song, though intellectually improbable, seems a wonderfully possible source for musical creation. In fact, to me the siren's song is the Holy Grail of musical appreciation as it not only captivates the listener with aural beauty but is also heard along the shores of bodies of water – to me the most hypnotic of environments.
    Music is essential to my life. I not only make music for a living, but I spend much of my day in search of sound that will bring on what I can only describe as a rush or high. I spend hours at music stores looking for musical treasures. One of my favorite activities is looking through the bargain bins of record stores for the hidden treasures. I know of a music store that sells fifty CDs for ten dollars. I weed through these recordings of mostly unknown artists and demo recordings for the transcendent musical moment:

a unique voice, an interesting pairing of instruments like a trombone and harp, or a curious combination of chords. I get a burst of aliveness that more than anything else in life brings tears to my eyes. I feel myself awaken completely to the beauty of being alive within my human skin. This is as good as it gets for me. I hold on to these musical memories for days until they begin to fade, and then I am compelled to look for the next musical fix. I crave music. I am addicted to it.

Being near water has a similar affect. As I live by the ocean, it is usually this body of water that I immerse myself in (kayaking, swimming, surfing) almost daily. Unlike other addictions that can be abused and lead to unhealthy physical conditions (gaunt face, needle marks, extended gut), my addiction to water often cures me of physical ailments and creates in me an incredible sense of physical health. I have come home from work completely exhausted and feeling on the verge of the flu, immersed myself in the water of the Pacific Ocean near my home and returned miraculously recovered, literally feeling like a new man. People say it is the negative ions, or the brisk coldness of the 50-something degree water. Whatever it is, I yearn for this revitalization and actually feel completely out of sorts if I do not have access to this ritual dousing. This can be inconvenient and uncomfortable on my trips inland, driving on freeways through dry parched land with no access to large vistas of open water. These roads don't take me to where I want to go. My body seems to suffer withdrawal, and I feel physically weak and emotionally cranky.

Like the most capable drug-dealer, the siren myth has the potential to offer a source for my two addictions: beautiful music within the confines of water. Thus when the fates aligned and offered me a Bolivian adventure paddling the waters of Lake Titicaca with my friend Justin in search of a siren's song, I found myself powerless to resist.

To go on this trip I would need a few essential items, a kayak to travel by and a musical instrument that could somehow capture and interpret the siren's song. If I were lucky enough to somehow hear one, I didn't want to record it with machinery but with something that creates music itself. I chose the South American

My lovely much-used charango

ten-stringed *charango* for reasons I will explain later in the introduction. It was also important to embark on this adventure with a balance of open-mindedness and a strong sense of humor. I only need to look at my children to see a template for this point of view. Watching them interact with monsters, aliens and talking wild animals shows me that anything is possible if looked at through the lens of lightness on this earth. A park is filled with the laughter and singsong voices of humans interacting creatively with the world around them. I don't expect a lecture from my kids on the dogma of sandbox creatures; I only expect the incredible vision of dirty knees, sand in the hair and the knowing smiles of the infinite possibilities of a human's capacity for wildness and imagination.

It All Started...

1
Charangos

The *charango* is my favorite instrument – the one possession I cherish most in the world. So what exactly is a charango, and why do I love it so much? A charango is an Andean ten-stringed instrument made out of wood, or sometimes out of a *Tatu-mulita*'s (armadillo's) armored shell. The charango has a somewhat comical appearance because it has a very small body with a long neck capped at the end with ten tuning pegs. The tuning pegs take up a third of the instrument. It's the platypus of guitars. Whenever I take my charango out to play for kids under the age of five, they almost always laugh at it. Even more dramatic and perhaps humorous is the intensity and speed with which great *charanguistas* play their instruments. It's a good instrument for me as it is melodic, good for songwriting, and it also allows me to play at the speed that matches my energy, which is usually spastic.

I bought my first charango in La Paz, Bolivia in 1992, and it was truly love at first touch. The first time I played a well-made charango, I was hooked for life. The owner grabbed my index finger and placed it on the strings covering the sound hole and told me to "*RASGASTESE* (trill) *rápido...RÁPIDO*...Damn you gringo, faster!!" I have finally gotten a handle on manic "trilling" (my hand now looks like a blur when I play) and the charango has been a huge part of my life ever since.

The best tones from the trilling finger are achieved by growing the fingernail out so it acts as a pick. The index fingernails of the charango players I have met all had the same thick, almost hoof-like nail (yikes!) for maximum trilling potential. It took me many years to develop such a tough resilient nail. At first my nail would often break off right at the skin, which was not only painful, but made trilling hard. I would then be rubbing raw skin on the surface of the strings, which very much dulled the acoustic properties of the strings, and also gave me painful blisters on the tips of my fingers. I love the fact that the first thing I look at when meeting a fellow charango player is his index nail. The more gnarled the nail looks, the more respect I have for him or her.

The charango's unique high pitched, ten-stringed sound was inspired by the Spanish *vihuela and Guitarra espanola*, brought over during the "conquest" in the 1700s. Other instruments that influenced its shape and construction are the *bandurria* (mandolin) and lute. There are many small stringed instruments played in the Americas that have similar European backgrounds, such as the *ukulele, cuatro* and *cavaquinho.* It is always amazing to me that when played, these instruments evoke the characteristics of their countries of origin. Much has to do with the rhythms and melodies that are played on them, which match the cultures' own sensibilities. The Brazilian *cavaquinho* strums a samba beat with chords filled with *saudade* (a uniquely Brazilian melancholy) while the ukulele sounds like the tropical sandy beaches of Waikiki, with its slow, swaying rhythms and comforting chords.

When I play the charango, I am sometimes asked if I am from the Andes, as this instrument is not commonly played in the United States. Those asking might just be curious, but sometimes my insecurities turn their question into "How can you play something so obviously not part of your cultural background?" This, of course, is absurd on many levels. If cultural heritage is a prerequisite for playing instruments, what would I be allowed to play? The kazoo? Because my cultural heritage is a mosaic of Europe, U.S. and Brazil, does this mean I can only play music from these areas? Of course not! The cultural identity of musical instruments is also often very complex, as instruments have had to cross many cultural barriers to exist in their current form. There are African, Asian and European roots to most of the instruments we play in symphonies, jazz, bluegrass and rock bands. Still, whenever I play the charango, I can hear the Andean landscape from which it came, regardless of what music I play on it. Perhaps the particular wood smell reminds me of the *altiplano,* the Andean Highlands.

When I first traveled through the altiplano region of the Andes, I was impressed by the silence of the land, a silence only broken by the mysterious moans of a wind that has practically no boundaries, as much of the land is virtually tree-less. The sound of the wind blowing through the high plains is truly mystical, and is, in fact, wonderfully recreated through the sounds of many Andean folk music instruments. Just as regional languages have specific definitions for their own unique landscape, musical instruments have been developed and used like language to express the uniqueness of a particular environment. The environment becomes the "collaborator" in musical creation. For example, the Andean *zampoñas* (panpipes) beautifully evoke the windy sounds of the *altiplano*; the *bombo* drum is the thunder that rocks the earth; and *chak'jas* rattles represent the rains sucked up by the dry earth. The charango adds another element to the Andean musical sound, the sound of the *sirena*, water spirit or siren.

2
The Andean *Sirena*

The *sirena* is a bewitching figure in many cultures, and that is no exception in the Andes. It is believed by some that the Andean charango, if placed by a water source, can catch the siren's song within its strings and body and bewitch not only the charango player, but the audience as well.

I first heard about the sirens or *sirenas* in the Andean mountains from a wonderful music professor and Andean scholar named John Schechter, while studying with him at U.C. Santa Cruz. He gave me an article written by the ethnomusicologist Thomas Turino about sirenas and charangos in Peru and Lake Titicaca. This article, entitled "The Charango and the *Sirena*: Music, Magic and the Power of Love," told of the belief that the charango, as used by rural people specifically in Southern Peru, can capture the entrancing music of the water spirits (sirenas) inhabiting the altiplano region. The most common belief is that the sirena will play the charango if it is placed overnight near a particular place where sirenas sing. The sirena plays the charango, giving it perfect pitch and a magical entrancing sound, much like the songs of the sirens themselves. Thomas Turino himself had an experience along the shore of Lake Titicaca. After playing his charango for a while, he rested it on his lap and soon noticed a unique ringing sound, a "celestial tonic" coming from the instrument. At first he thought it must be the wind vibrating the strings, but when he tried on numerous occasions to recreate the same sound on equally windy days along the lake and in his hotel, holding his charango in numerous positions, he was never able to duplicate the magical sound. When he explained this to a local villager, the villager knowingly and enthusiastically replied that the location where he had had his unexplainable musical experience was next to a well known home of a sirena! This intriguing anecdote, sandwiched in the prose of an academic ethnographic journal, this chink in the armor of academic subjectivity, captured my imagination. In this beautiful lake high in the Andean mountains, I could hear the siren's song calling to me from thousands of miles away.

After reading Turino's article, I was inspired to write a song called *Nuevo Charango* (New Charango), about siren songs entering my charango from the Pacific Ocean's waves that pound the cliffs in front of the tiny apartment my wife and I were renting on Seabright Beach in Santa Cruz. I would play the charango by the shores for hours, and later at night in my apartment I would listen to hear the sounds of the ocean within the strings. I wondered if sirens' songs could be caught within the strings without the process of leaving the instrument out overnight for them to play as was described in the article. If I were to leave my charango overnight in Santa Cruz, I probably would never see it again as it would most likely disappear into the backseat of a very non-sirena-like late-night beach partier!

Later, recording a live version of this song with my engineer friend Pete, something very interesting occurred. We were set up on the beach by the high tide line, trying to get as close to the crashing waves as possible without getting wet. I wanted to record the song on the beach with the sounds of the waves playing over the strumming of the charango. As he set up the recording gear, I looked up at the blue sky and saw a few windswept clouds heading our way. He gave me a thumbs-up, and I began to play the charango. Within a minute of playing, it began to sprinkle. I looked up, and those few clouds had converged just over our heads and created a mini rainstorm. We laughed at the absurdity of the chances of this happening. Here we were, singing a song in the dry early summer about water spirits and it begins to rain...seemingly only on us... at the beginning of the song. The rain stopped abruptly, and we recorded the song in its entirety, but with the sweetness of the water still glistening on the charango. A good omen, I thought. I wrote this song in Spanish, and the chorus translates:

Music made of wood, and chords of the heart
A romance of two countries, two waters mixing
And here inside, a mysterious chorus
Two voices singing the love of the sirenas

I knew I had to go to Bolivia to complete this chorus of sirenas. I wanted to go to Lake Titicaca where Thomas Turino had visited and experienced the unexplainable. An idea formed in my head – I needed to take a musical kayak trip to Lake Titicaca to entertain the possibility of capturing a siren song in my charango.

3
My Travel Partner

I had planned to visit Lake Titicaca with my friend Greg, as we have a standing agreement to create an adventure together every year if at all possible. We were friends during high school and college, playing soccer, surfing, climbing and enjoying the adventures of life. Now that we had families and lived in different states, it was much harder to get together, so we made plans to meet each other every year for an adventure. Thankfully both wives and families agreed, knowing that these trips are so important to us. It also got us out of their hair for a short while. As sometimes happens with friends who have families, a few months before we were to leave, Greg told me he wouldn't be able to go to Bolivia. Finances, kids going to camp, sick babies, etc. He just couldn't make it this year. As this was a trip I had wanted to make for many years, I didn't want to cancel, so I decided to find a new travel partner. Luckily, I found a perfect travel mate in Justin.

Finding travel partners can be tricky. This will be the person with whom you will share intense experiences…illnesses and misfortunes such as dysentery, sunstroke, snakebites; getting lost, shipwrecked, shanghaied, robbed or drunk on strange and dubious local alcoholic beverages; and, on the other hand, enjoy the pleasures inherent in travel such as viewing pristine mountains and hidden beaches, sampling distinctive (and cheap!) foods, and immersing oneself in wonderful and rich cultures. Having a person who reacts in a similar way as you do during these experiences can be vital. I wanted a person with a good sense of humor, an openness to dive headfirst into the unknown, and, for this trip in particular, a leaving behind of cynicism. This trip entailed searching for a siren's song, for goodness sake, and I wanted a person willing to believe in, or at least not to laugh too hard at my siren-searching endeavors.

Justin is a perfect combination of all of these things. He is a fourth grade teacher and has two young kids of his own; the eldest is one of my son's best friends. He appreciates what it is like to have childlike wonder as he is immersed in it every day. We had surfed together as well and shared the joys of the ocean. Justin understands the power of water and was drawn to the siren's call of waves crashing against the cliffs. He had also traveled to South America before and was familiar with the languages and customs of the region, and the potential for even the best laid plans to need spontaneous adjustment. He is also a musician. I also knew he was on summer vacation, so the timing of the trip might be right for him. Now all I had to do was convince him to come....I was amazed with our first conversation, which played out something like this:

"Hey, Justin what's up?"

"Not much, and you?"

"Not much...hey, would you like to go Bolivia to search and listen for siren's songs in a kayak?"

"Sure, why not."

Then the better part of him (the sane part) decided it would be a good idea to talk this over with his family, so he said that he would get back to me as soon as possible. Then came the wait. After about a week of no further communication, I started to realize how odd and perhaps frivolous this trip might seem to some, and I began to have doubts about him wanting to come. I left Justin a message that I was going to buy a ticket for myself, and that I had reserved a ticket for him as well if he wanted. I didn't get a call back, and after leaving a few more messages I was resigned to the fact that I would be making this trip by myself. Just when I had rearranged in my brain what a solo trip would be like, I got a call from Justin. He not only wanted to go but had bought an airplane ticket on his own. We would arrive on different days (him earlier than me), but we would be returning on the same flight. So after splitting up the folding kayak into two bags and making lists of other trip necessities such as tents, stoves, warm clothes and lots and lots of sunscreen, the trip was finally a go!

The Perfect Charango

1
Arriving

I left from San Francisco Airport on a foggy July morning and arrived at the tropically humid Miami International Airport five hours later. Miami is the major staging point for many Latin American destinations, and you can see why. You are treated differently. There is more joking, and a sort of Latin rhythm to the proceedings. Things take a little bit longer. More people are sweating, and there is less clothing. There is more yelling, in a friendly way. The food is different – I had black beans and rice while waiting for my flight, and my dessert was rice pudding with coconut in it. Of course much more Spanish was spoken, and there were many shades of brown walking from flight to flight. For me, it was a nice sendoff to a land where many of my roots, influences and points of view originate. I was flying into a continent that is directly related to my birth (Brazilian mom), my musical career, my wife (we met playing in a Latin American music recital), the name of my son (his middle name is Caetano after a well-known Brazilian singer), and, of course, the amazing dance moves my skinny white legs are famous for (in my mind).

This trip was finally happening. The boat, a two-person *folboat* kayak, and my camping gear were all tucked away (hopefully) in the belly of the plane, and I sat in my seat waiting to land in La Paz, Bolivia. It was a strange time to travel in many ways. My wife and I were due to have our second child in a month and a half, and she assured me it would not come early, but I still felt nervous. While it was true that this trip would be less likely to happen after the baby was born, I was feeling guilty as I imagined friends and family discussing my flight from the nest as my eight-month pregnant wife waddled uncomfortably around the house preparing for our new baby. Such a selfish bastard! And to cavort with mermaids no less!

As the plane filled up, my excitement grew. The other people getting on the plane were an interesting mix of missionaries (large, loud white men with computers and baseball hats), young travelers (scraggly types carrying backpacks with many dangling attachments) and Latin Americans returning home or going to visit relatives. As I unfortunately don't look that young anymore and didn't have a computer or baseball hat, I tried to give off the air of an international explorer in search of secrets of world importance, a Charles Darwin, Dian Fossey, or Sir Edmund Hillary. This impression was probably slightly diminished as I intently watched "Spongebob Squarepants" on the individual movie screen in front of me.

In-flight meals have changed over the years. No more all you can drink free beer and decent meals. Many years before on a flight to South America, I drank six free beers with a crazy Venezuelan who kept trying to convince me to go to his home in Caracas to start a business selling Harley Davidson motorcycles. These drunken experiences provided free from the airlines are no more. The flight from the U.S had no food at all, unless you paid for a deli-wrap sandwich for ten bucks. I couldn't buy the sandwich even if I wanted to, due to stresses on my body from other gastronomical exploits in Latin America (tape worm, giardia, burst appendix) which have left my body unable to tolerate wheat or gluten in my diet. I get a bloated stomach and headaches with just the tiniest bit of these substances. So I came armed with gluten-free snacks for the six and a half hour flight. Once, on a flight to Japan, I sat next to a very large man (obese actually) who had taken a quantity of sleeping pills before take off. He wasn't going to budge for the twelve-hour flight. After I had eaten the veggie cutlet offered on the plane, I soon realized that it contained wheat flour and that I was going to go through the torture of bloat supreme without access to the toilet which was now blocked by Mr. Large…hellish.

2
La Paz

The flight arrived in La Paz, Bolivia at 6:00 in the morning. I was a little nervous about arriving so early with all my bags after no sleep and having to slog it to the capital city of La Paz. But thanks to my traveling partner Justin, who arrived a day earlier, there was a man with a sign saying "Mr. Snyder" waiting at the terminal entrance. Never had one of those signs before. Mr. Snyder has arrived and has a sign… give the man some room! I pushed my way through the riffraff of people, poor minions who didn't have "people" waiting for them and stepped out into the cold Bolivian air.

The airport is at the top of a steep bowl valley that empties downward into La Paz, which at this early hour was still sleeping. Unfortunately, the sun had not risen, so I was not able to see the amazing snow-covered 24,000 foot peaks surrounding me. The thin, cool air reminded me that I was quite high up as well, a difference of 12,500 feet from my home along the northern California coast.

I arrived at the arranged hotel hoping to find my friend. It was a small but friendly hotel near the city center. I ran up the stairs, stumbled at the top and asked the receptionist in a voice not quite mine (the altitude and tiredness gave me a gargoyle like rasp) if my friend was in. Justin heard me through the prerequisite paper-thin walls of the traveler hotel, and met me at the front desk. We hugged quickly, and then I ran back down and paid the cab driver (insulting him by thinking that the thirty minute cab ride was six *Bolivianos*, 80 cents, rather than six dollars). I ran back upstairs with my stuff, disregarding the warning signals from my oxygen-deprived brain to slow down. Justin knowingly offered me some water, as he had the same dry rasp upon arriving the day before, and we grinned at each other. The trip had officially begun.

Justin had made it with no problems, and as he was carrying half of our folding boat, we now had a whole boat, which is important for any successful kayak trip! Today we would find the instruments we would later play to the water spirits of Lake Titicaca. The following day we would head for the lakeside city of Copacabana, our starting point for the kayak journey to the Isla del Sol and Isla de la Luna. We had decided to buy instruments for the trip after our arrival in La Paz, rather than bring our own from home, for a number of reasons. It was more baggage to carry on the plane, but most importantly we wanted instruments that could possibly get wet, and didn't want the chance of ruining our precious instruments from home.

3
Charango Day

Before we could look for instruments to take on the trip (charango for me and guitar for Justin), we needed some breakfast. We especially wanted some tea – coca leaf tea to be exact. Coca leaves are known to alleviate the headache and fatigue of high altitude, and I remembered them working for me years earlier on my previous trip to Bolivia – and they're tasty as well. I was really feeling the high elevation as just a few steps made my head throb. We found a small breakfast place in the lobby of our hotel filled with travelers and dined on fruits, eggs, and large mugs of coca leaves in hot water with honey. Its nutty, earthy taste was as marvelous as I had remembered and I hoped it would do something to alleviate this headache that was increasing in severity by the minute.

With my empty mug of tea, with left over green coca leaves pasted to the side, off we went. We walked into the area sometimes called in the guidebooks "Gringo Alley" because of its high density of traveler hotels and artisan shops. Beautiful handmade traditional textiles were being sold along the streets where men and women stood over piles of ponchos and shawls woven in wonderful earth tones that seemed to be dug right out of the earth. Alpaca and llama sweaters were also displayed, their popularity illustrated by the throngs of tourists who wore them throughout the city. We would, of course, join these ranks and buy our fill of products, but not until we returned from the kayak trip. Our kayak would be filled to capacity as it was, but there was room for one more important item, a charango.

Charangos are considered by many Bolivians to be the national instrument. They are proudly displayed in storefront windows along with the names of the luthiers who created the instruments. The charangos I was looking for were not made from armadillos, as many traditionally have been, as the armadillo has unfortunately been hunted to endangered status. Although you can still find these

Street vendors in La Paz

armadillo charangos, called *quirquincho,* hanging illicitly from storefront walls, I was looking for the ones made from a variety of woods, imparting each charango with a distinctive tone.

Gringo Alley is a paradise of charangos, but you have to know what to look for. Stores have hundreds of charangos, but there are only a few really great ones that are exceptionally made. The good ones are usually displayed high up, behind glass, or anywhere where the unqualified hands of tourists can't touch them. It was almost like courting the daughter of a patriarch from a Gabriel Garcia Marquez book as some stores outright forbade me from playing or even looking at some of the higher end models. It was true many tourists wanted the charango to put on their wall along with other trinkets from their world travels, and the cheaply-made twenty-five dollar charangos would do fine for them. But I was looking for something much more, a charango whose tone would allure a sirena to play it along the shores of Lake Titicaca!

4
The Perfect Charango

We walked through dozens of stores looking for the perfect instrument. There was one in particular where I had bought my first charango the last time I was in La Paz. The charango I bought there many years ago was amazing and was my first really high quality instrument. I had bought it used from a charango master (or so they said), and it really did have an amazing tone. I knew it was a work of art after the first strum, which is all I could muster the first time playing it. The sound seemed to ring and expand inside me. I'd never held a musical instrument of such craftsmanship before, so I wanted another charango from the same shop if possible. As I couldn't remember the exact location of the shop, Justin and I went in search for it, hidden somewhere in Gringo Alley.

There was a dilemma in my choice of charango. If I bought a truly great, and probably expensive one for the trip, there was a chance that it could get wet and ruined as we kayaked around the lake. So I decided to buy two charangos, a cheaper model for the kayak trip with a good enough sound, and when the trip was over, I would return to buy the more expensive "work of art" charango, taking both charangos back home with me. I eventually found a perfect one for the trip in a small store with a friendly owner who was the actual creator of the instruments, not just a salesman. It was not the shop where I had bought my previous charango, but I was immediately drawn inside because of its walls of exquisite-looking instruments. I tried five or six charangos when my eyes caught one that had a slightly different look, not as rounded as most, almost guitar-like. Cradled in my arms, it sat on my chest differently than my charango at home. It is such an intimate, sensual experience to play an instrument for the first time, like a first kiss. The more I played it, the more I fell in love with it. It was a hidden beauty. It didn't have as rich a sound as the one I had bought fifteen years before, but none of the ones in the store did. The owner explained that perhaps my previous charango was made of wood such as the Bolivian rosewood or *palo santo*, which is not as available because of over-harvesting. That was sad, but I was excited that I had found a new charango "voice" for our trip to the islands of Lake Titicaca. The distinctive sounds that different woods can produce in musical instruments was a new awareness for me, and with charangos I was really starting to take note. In general, the woods that were darker had a warmer tone that I liked, whereas the lighter woods had a bright ring that the native players seemed to enjoy.

It was pure bliss playing dozens of charangos and finally coming to that special one that resonated so well throughout my body. Finding it to be of one of the more inexpensive models was also a plus. I knew that this would be the perfect charango for the trip and perhaps even a home for a siren's song from Lake Titicaca.

Justin also bought a guitar from the same friendly luthier that was also inexpensive, but had a shape and sound that intrigued him. It was much skinnier than the usually nylon-stringed guitar, maybe six inches in width, but it still had a deep, full sound. When we told him we would be carrying the guitar on top of our boat, as it wouldn't fit inside, he looked shocked, as though we were telling him we would be shortly setting it on fire. We bought a cloth case to ease his disappointment in us and to protect the guitar from splashing water. I bought a more sturdy, hard case for the charango and actually planned on putting it inside a waterproof bag. I wasn't taking any chances on ruining it.

I told many of the more friendly music storeowners that I met about my interest in charangos and water spirits of the lake. Thankfully, most knew what I was talking about and repeated similar beliefs that I had read about in Thomas Turino's article. One man laughed and snidely pronounced, "You mean the song of the Diablo (devil)?" I had heard about this interpretation as well. The charango left overnight in specific locations lures out the devil, who then plays it, leaving powers of seduction within its wooden body. This description is much like the ones I had read about with the sirenas, except the "devil" method of entrancement seemed more dubious. The charango player begins to play the devil's song on the charango, and women then become powerless to resist the advances of the wooing musician. It sounded like a musical violation, especially as the storeowner and his buddies laughed sinisterly as they spoke of this interpretation. The sirena/charango story had been translated from my eco-spiritual ideal into frat party conversation. On the bright side, at least I wasn't met with blank stares, as was always a possibility.

5
Altitude Sickness

Outfitted with our instruments, we headed back to the hotel to meet up with a good friend's Christina's cousin Bernie, who lives in La Paz. He had been very helpful to us before our arrival, answering the questions in our e-mails and agreeing to be our contact person here in Bolivia in case of an emergency. He invited us to dinner the night before we headed out. We met him in the hotel, and he took us to a restaurant where we could "explain ourselves."

"The sun is *insoportable* (unbearable) in the day, and the weather is freezing in the night. Do you know what you are getting yourselves into?" he asked.

"What happens if you flip over?"

"Did you bring a radio in case you get into trouble?"

"How will you eat?"

He asked these questions with true concern in his eyes. He wanted to make sure we had prepared ourselves and knew what we were getting ourselves into. We looked as confident as we could, but we all knew the true answer – which is true with all adventures – who knows?

At the restaurant Bernie chose, we described our interesting culinary restrictions. The fact that Justin was a vegetarian (he did eat fish) was confusing, but the fact that I could not eat wheat was beyond confusing and entered the territory of freakishness.

Special diets is such a part of culture in the United States that we forget it is not such a luxury in other parts of the world. The fact that I couldn't and wouldn't eat bread was astounding to our host and probably unthinkable to much of the world. Bread is the substance of life, the main food in prisons and a sacred food in churches. "Breaking the Bread" would not be a religious experience for me, but a sign to ask to be excused from the table.

We all finally did find something to eat and continued to talk about the trip. We reassured him of our experience in kayaking, and how we had mapped out our trip in advance (more or less), all while giving off the airs of great adventurers, which, of course, we considered ourselves. We informed him of our estimated date of return to La Paz and asked if he would check up on us if we did not show up within a few days of this date. As he had a car, he told us he could drive to Lake Titicaca within three hours and that he would also come looking for us if there was an emergency back home. He also told us ominously that the local press had written of a possible worker strike in El Alto, a city just north of La Paz, where blockades could prohibit all vehicles from entering or leaving La Paz. I could just imagine Justin and me laden with kayaks and paddles trying to sneak by angry workers shouting in megaphones about injustices, pleading with them to let us through so we could play music with sirenas. I'm sure they would understand the urgency of our vitally important quest and let us through!

During the meal, my altitude sickness became more pronounced as I slurred my speech and dropped my fork on the floor, not once, but four times. Each time, the restaurant owner dutifully got me a new one. I wondered how many forks would he give me; could I continue with this all night? Our Bolivian friend looked on with great concern for my well-being, his worried eyes conveying the possibility of hospitalization. Justin seemed concerned as well. More coca tea was all I could think about. Was this the beginning of an addiction? Would I be mainlining coca leaf paste next?

After dinner, he wouldn't let us go back to the hotel until we had gone to the local pharmacy to buy anti-*soroche* (altitude sickness) medicine, and made sure I took some. He then hailed us a taxi and wished us luck on our trip. He was such a kind and helpful person, we sincerely hoped we would not need him to rescue us.

Copacabana

1
Heading Off

Early the next morning, we feasted again on eggs, papaya and coca leaf tea. I do love this tea, and I considered filling up a canteen for all day consumption. Actually, many people bypass the whole tea experience (takes too much time, perhaps) for simply putting coca leaves directly into their mouths. Many of the street venders had huge mouthfuls of the stuff. It had the potential to look very unsightly, like humans chewing cud, but the blissful gaze and mellow demeanor these people exuded only made me wonder why we weren't all doing the same thing.

Fully nourished, we gathered all of our belongings and headed out into the street, looking absolutely absurd carrying bag after bag of kayak, backpacks, paddles and instruments. We felt so North American, so fat with wealth, with our giant mound of stuff. We couldn't wait to unfold our kayak at the lake and pack all of our gear inside so that we could be self-contained. A wonderful attribute of kayak travel is the ability to pack all the gear into the boat, rather than on your back.

Kayaks in the Arctic region have been adapted over hundreds of years to transport huge loads such as hunted seals and walruses and have even carried whole families within the sealskin hull. Our traveling kayak made by *Folbot* fit into two bags weighing a total of 62 pounds. When assembled, it can carry up to 600 pounds of weight. The kayak's double-bladed paddle, perfectly designed over hundreds of years, efficiently pulls this large weight through the water with surprisingly little effort from the rower.

After loading all our gear into a taxi heading for the bus terminal to Lake Titicaca, our taxi driver told us about his sirena story when I mentioned what we would be doing on our trip. He got a joyous look on his face and said one has to have *fe* (faith), as there really are sirenas that sing and enchant via instruments. Interestingly, he said this not only happens by water and gave an example. His family brought their instruments out to the altiplano next to specific "power places" he called *huaca*s and left them there over night. In the morning their instruments sounded better, or as happened to him, the player suddenly played much better. He said he had always wanted to play the trumpet as a kid but couldn't get a tone from it. He blew hard, his big face turning red as he demonstrated his futile attempts as a child. So one day, he put his trumpet out over night by the *huaca*, and in the morning in front of his father he played his trumpet with wonderful, clear notes. Again he mimed playing the trumpet for us, face turning bright red, with a huge smile on his face. His whole family was amazed.

I loved his use of the word *fe* to describe this episode of his life. It was his faith, and his family's faith, that created this opportunity to have the environment sing through the trumpet. Faith that the special place in the altiplano would help him. It was a spiritual experience for him. His eyes sparkled with the memory. He wished us good luck at the lake with the sirenas. He knew they would come.

2
The Bus Ride

The trip to Copacabana, the starting point for our kayak trip, is about a four-hour bus ride from La Paz. At the bus terminal we saw three different buses heading to Copacabana, all different sizes: a minivan, a minibus and a regular-sized bus. They all said they were leaving when the buses were full, and since the minivan seemed the smallest, we figured it would be filled up first – a poor and uneducated choice on our part. The minivan was much smaller, but without us knowing, they were going to fill it up to its utmost limit. I mean FILL IT UP. Bags of peanuts, clothing, suitcases, backpacks and kayaks were lifted up onto the roof, and then like so many cattle, we were herded in. The end result was a ten-person minibus fitting seventeen, three of whom had to sit on the floor by the front door. Unfortunately I ended up being one of these floor people. Initially I had a nice seat, but I got out to go to the outhouse on the street (for future reference, not recommended), and upon my return, saw that my seat had been taken by a very uncooperative Brazilian woman. She had gotten on the bus in my absence and had taken my seat (with protests from the other passengers), even though the seats were already assigned. She wouldn't budge, and I wasn't in the mood for arguing. The girl from Ipanema this wasn't. The Bolivians on the bus even gave her stinkface. I like the Bolivians!

I find that the Bolivian people in general possess a wonderful blend of humility and generosity. The stark landscape seems to have cut away some of the more self-indulgent human traits, replacing them with a humble stoicism. This might stem from the hardships of daily life and the oppression that the (roughly two-thirds) indigenous population have endured through three centuries of colonial rule and destabilizing revolutions. During the Spanish conquest of the region, the native cultures were forced into brutal, exhausting, and sometimes deadly labor to extract the land's riches, most significantly silver, to be transported back to Europe.

Bolivia gained independence from Spain in 1825 but has weathered much political instability since then. In its history, Bolivia has experienced over 150 *coup-de-etats*, which is actually a world record. Most famously, the global icon of revolution, Che Guevara, died in the Bolivian mountains in 1967 with his meager group of followers, who tried unsuccessfully to rally the Bolivians into guerrilla warfare against the U.S.-backed Bolivian military.

Through these unstable times, Bolivians have maintained their strong cultural identity. This proud cultural endurance is wonderfully illustrated by the fact that the majority of the population speaks indigenous languages. In particular *Aymara* and *Quechua*, which are some of the few native languages in the world that are growing in numbers of speakers. It is always humbling to travel through this country realizing that most people are completely bilingual and often trilingual speakers (*Spanish/Aymara/Quechua*). This does not even include the language *Guarani*, which is spoken mostly in the lowlands near the tropical forests.

Back in the bus with my coveted seat lost, I sat on the engine cover scrunched up next to a very sweet older Aymara-speaking couple (they could have been in there 80s or 40s – hard to tell). They smiled at me with mouths full of coca leaves, and the resultant green teeth. As the trip progressed, we leaned up against one another as if we were family. I actually felt very lucky to be practically in the laps of these Bolivians as we passed through the beautiful *altiplano* countryside with small villages constructed of mud, llamas grazing, and the snow capped *Cordillera Real* range always on the horizon. For the whole four and a half hours, we kept smiling at each other. The Brazilian woman lost out on this opportunity and got scowls from us all. Bus karma.

We finally arrived at Lake Titicaca in the port village of San Pedro where we would ferry our minibus to the other side of the peninsula that led to Copacabana, an hour's drive away. The other side of this peninsula is also where part of the Bolivian navy is stationed. Although landlocked, Bolivia still keeps this military branch functioning in case the long stretch of the Pacific Ocean coast lost to Chile in the war of 1879–1883 is returned. The loss of coastline to the Chileans is still a sore spot for Bolivians that is lamented every year on March 23rd, Bolivian Sea Day, a surprising holiday for the visiting tourist (what sea?), but a hopeful one for Bolivians.

As we waited for our bus to make it across the twenty-minute ferry ride, I saw a man with a charango and asked him if he knew of any charango/sirena stories. It was such a strange encounter. I was so excited that the sirena belief seemed to be relatively well-known in La Paz that I assumed any person with a charango would now be a potential source for information and stories. So hurrying across the small town plaza, I approached the man like a deranged movie star's fan.

If I put myself in this man's shoes, I really must have looked odd. An obvious tourist runs huffing and puffing towards him away from the clump of tourists he *should* be with, questioning him with an altitude-sickness-induced raspy borderline creepy voice, about charango*s*, sirenas and "special" places. An appropriate analogy would be if someone from another country and culture walked down my street, gasping for air, and because I live in northern California, frantically asked me if I had ever come across Bigfoot.

Traveling seems to bring out my audacity. Once while paddling with my friend in Malaysia, we had run out of food due to lack of planning and were looking for breakfast in a small "gypsy" fishing village. We were tired, sunburned, smelly and dressed in shabby paddling shorts and t-shirts. The only applicable words we knew were *"Makan pagi"* literally "breakfast," and we walked down the dirt road blurting these words to anyone in earshot. Amazingly, we were led to a home where a savior of a woman cooked us a delicious breakfast. I couldn't imagine the same thing happening on my own street, with random strangers yelling "breakfast" and being invited inside to eat one. Probably the absurdity of it all made it intriguing enough to risk our company.

Back in Bolivia, the startled man very kindly listened to my jumbled question, and said there was a place at Copacabana where people put their charangos called *"Boca del sapo"* (mouth of the frog). He didn't say if he himself had taken his charango there and, looking slightly embarrassed, didn't elaborate further on the topic. I, on the other hand, was thrilled to actually have a name of a place, a *huaca*. I ran excitedly back to our bus, as the startled man shuffled away quickly. To the observer it must have looked like a drug transaction. I had a place, a location and an official sirena site now. This was exciting!

The city of Copacabana

The drive to Copacabana hardly took any time at all, and soon we saw the lake, startling blue and immense, lapping at the shores of this picturesque city. Copacabana, a city of perhaps 20,000 people, gives a jolt to the senses. After driving through the earth tones of the altiplano, it feels like arriving at an amusement park. Many of the homes have whitewashed walls, colorful blue or red window frames, and spectacularly arched doorways with Spanish tiles. Business and tourism seemed to be thriving: streets filled with hotels, restaurants, tourist shops and street vendors selling everything from fresh vegetables and fruits to track suits and DVD's of "Baywatch." Most visually spectacular is the giant baroque Moorish-influenced cathedral located in the city central. The white-domed roof can be seen for miles away, and the surrounding buildings and plaza take up a city block.

3
Copacabana Memories

I had been to this beautiful cathedral before with a group of six friends (including my future wife) in 1992. Leaving from Santa Cruz, California, we were on a six-month musical tour of South America in a brightly-colored van (purple and yellow) with sea turtles painted along the sides. It looked like Ken Keesey's magic bus crossed with Jacques Cousteau's *Calypso*. We had stopped off in Copacabana to partake in an interesting ritual we had read about in a tourist manual, the blessing of the vehicle (called *ch'alla*) by the priest of the church. When we arrived, there was already a line of vehicles, cars, buses and vans waiting to be spiritually cleansed. It was like a car confessional with all the "sins" of the road manifested on the battered bodies of the vehicles. Trucks with their fenders dented up, cars with cracked windshield and deeply weathered transport trucks stood in line next to our funky hippie van. After spending many months traveling on roads with giant potholes, military checkpoints, precarious cliff edges and even sand dunes in the middle of the road, we understood the significance of any additional precautions for our safety. The priest's blessing of our van was an opportunity not to be missed or taken lightly.

There was quite a fanfare to the proceedings as vendors sold their wares (colorful crucifixes, postcards of Jesus with 3D blinking eyes, rosettes) to waiting pilgrims. There was a short window of time when the priest made his way out to the cars, and we hoped that he would have time to bless everyone's vehicles since some people had traveled very far for the ritual. The priest, a wonderful grey-haired man with a big smile, thankfully showed up on time and sprinkled holy water on our van, laughing at our purple sea turtles. His blessings seemed to work because we arrived in Buenos Aires without incident in time for Christmas, which had been our goal.

Copacabana was also the place where Gwynne and I had our fondest memories of the trip. We loved the beautiful lake

Moorish cathedral of Copacabana

and the craggy peaks of rocks that surrounded it. One night Gwynne and I broke from the group and climbed some hills over-looking the city of Copacabana to watch the sun set over the lake while cuddling and drinking Chilean *Concha de Toro* red wine. Out in the distance was Isla del Sol, looking spectacularly like Hawaii surrounded by the Himalayas. It was here that I first thought of kayaking on the lake. My first idea was to go completely around the lake, but in later years realized that this would take months. I hadn't yet gone to La Paz and picked up a charango, so the sirena/charango connection was still unknown to me. The draw to explore this immense lake further stayed hidden within me for fifteen years.

4
Copacabana *Otra Vez*

I was jolted from my previous memories of Copacabana when the bus screeched to a halt in a plaza close to the shores of Titicaca, where our gear was unceremoniously dumped from the bus. Within minutes, all of our gear, kayaks and backpacks were taken, oh so thankfully, by carrier bike to a hotel right on the shore of Lake Titicaca. From our hotel rooms we could see the immensity of this beautiful deep, blue lake. The most amazing deep, almost purple blues, contrasted with the barren brown slopes that run along the shore. The lake goes to depths of 1,000 feet and is the biggest high elevation body of water on the planet. It is over 100 miles long and fifty miles across at its widest point. After the long bus ride, it was literally a sea of tranquility.

At the edge of our window was a point of land where we believed after reviewing our not too accurate map was *Boca del Sapo* which was the place where, according to the man I had met earlier in the day, musicians from Copacabana often left their instruments overnight to gain mystical properties. In other words, a possible sirena hangout. As we looked at this gorgeous lake, it became abundantly clear that if sirens exist in the world, they would definitely want to live here. We decided to check out "mouth of the frog" the next morning when we began our paddle trip. We couldn't leave our instruments out there over night, as was the protocol, because it was too far from the hotel. We didn't feel comfortable leaving our instruments out over night so close to town because if our instruments were stolen, borrowed or broken, our search for sirenas would be over before it started. We decided to begin our true sirena experiments in places we could access easily from our camping sites, away from humanity.

Camping was supposed to be easy and free anywhere along the lake. However, I was anxious about theft. I have been robbed numerous times in my travels throughout Latin America. This is common, of course, in all parts of the world and a small price to pay for the thrill of exploration, but understandably these thefts can become a real nuisance.

One prized possession I had while living in Costa Rica for two and a half years as a Peace Corps volunteer was a cassette player sent by my friends back in the U.S. Playing music on my cassette player was priceless during the long, lonely days of the rainy season. I left one day to visit the capital city, San Jose, and came back to see the player had been taken. After replacing it, the same thing happened again...and again. It was a battle of wits to see if it was worth buying a new one knowing it would be stolen again. It seemed as if I was providing the region with free music players. In the end, I rationalized that perhaps this was a good tradeoff for living in the area and was my special offering to the communities surrounding me. I could just see them waiting for me to get on the bus as word spread that a free cassette player was now being offered at my house. First come, first served. On our Lake Titicaca trip we would be traveling by kayak with only the bare essentials, so we could ill afford to support the local economy with free stuff as I had done in Costa Rica.

We were hungry after our long bus trip, so with our gear safely

A room with a view – Copacabana

in the hotel, we looked for a place to eat. All along the shore of the lake were little tents selling *trucha* (lake trout) with adjacent picnic tables for the customers. These mini eateries were lined up one after another, selling trout in various flavors (garlic, tomato, battered, grilled). The famous *"trucha"* of Lake Titicaca that we had heard so much about in La Paz and read about in tourist guidebooks was definitely living up to its reputation. Pictures of the surprisingly large trout adorned every homemade sign, loudly advertising, "AT THIS PARTICULAR ESTABLISHMENT WE WILL BE SERVING *TRUCHA*, *TRUCHA* AND MORE *TRUCHA*!!! IF YOU ARE LOOKING FOR *TRUCHA*, YOU HAVE COME TO THE RIGHT PLACE!" We passed various tents looking for the right one. It was strange passing some completely empty tents selling trucha, while the tents next door were completely full of people eating exactly what was being offered in the empty tent. Trucha! We decided to go to one of the empty ones to give them some needed business.

An elderly woman came out and asked us what we wanted, which we assumed meant, "How do you want your trucha?" I explained that I wanted to have the trucha without flour, which I knew translated into *harina,* or more specifically *harina de trigo.* I pointed to the menu that read, *"trucha a la parrila con ajo,"* which I optimistically assumed meant grilled trout with garlic. She nodded quickly and blurted out the obligatory "Si" and returned within seconds (were they cooked or just being stored behind the counter?) with deeply fried and deeply battered trucha. I was left with a dilemma. Should I tell the lady I had requested no batter, no *harina*, or should I just try and peel off the batter and eat what little uncontaminated fish I could find, thus not creating a "scene?" As it was my first day here and I was starving, I decided to eat what I could. I didn't want my first interaction on the lake to be one of the obnoxious demanding foreigner who is never satisfied. It turned out the fish was so deep-fried that I was able to retrieve very little fish not covered in greasy batter. The more I battled the trucha to relinquish a morsel of uncontaminated meat, the more my mood darkened. So while Justin enjoyed his trucha by the lake, soaking in the marvelous view, I was silently fuming at a sweet old woman who had put some flour on my fish. I was going to have to make some adjustments to my traveler attitude.

5
Trip Philosophy

In the morning, we were ready to get food and gear necessary for our two-week excursion on the lake. We were planning to camp the entire time, so we needed enough water and food to last for much of the trip. Even though we would be close to some villages, we wanted to be away from civilization for most of the trip. This way we could explore our spiritual and adventurous sides without guidelines or guidance from outside sources. It's something like going to church without priests or doctrine dictating spirituality, just being allowed to sit in silence enjoying the majesty of marble columns, stained glass windows, incense and candles. The silence and solitude of a space often leads to the deepest personal insights.

The vision I had for our journey was to be on deserted beaches looking for caves and rocks which seemed magical enough to entice sirenas to come and play our instruments. I wanted to get up in the morning and hear the voice of the sirena captured in the musical vibrations of the charango's strings. I wanted a musical "fix" I have never experienced before...like hearing the Beatles for the first time, or the first laugh uttered from my son Liam because of a silly face I made. In order to do this, we would have to suspend our middle-aged cynical beliefs for a while. One theme of this trip was to re-open a part of me that believed in magical happenings, especially in nature. For much of my twenties I was very open to the mysteries of nature and felt deeply moved and altered by exploring the natural world. In those times, I felt and experienced things that would not have happened if I had not met them with an open mind. Doors to other realms of consciousness opened up to me. How could they not while I swam with pink dolphins in the Amazon River, camped overnight on Temple Seven in Tikal National Park in Guatemala, watched hundreds of sea turtles nest in one night on a Costa Rican beach, or experienced an eighty-foot long finback whale pass directly underneath my surfboard in Baja, California? These images helped me to understand our earth's capacity to astound and also led me to look for the smaller, less dramatic wonders as well. Beneath the whale's fins and on the jungle floor next to ancient ruins are countless worlds of beauty that become more accessible when we take the time to look for them.

It was not as easy anymore to have "wild" and adventurous experiences. Life, mortgage, car problems, comforts – you know the story. I wasn't throwing myself into the *outside* world as much, and it showed in my forty-four-year-old outlook on life. I seemed to have covered up a bit of this access to wildness, *my* wildness, and I wanted it back. I wanted to feel the magic I knew that came with immersion in wild places. I wanted the part of me that mocked anything "new-agey" to stop being so damn cynical. My life was filled with a wonderful family and a satisfying job, but somewhere along the line, I had lost contact with my knowledge of magic unseen in one's surroundings. I found myself walking past flowers and interesting rocks. Our families had thankfully given Justin and me an opportunity to become re-acquainted with this part of ourselves. Thank you, families. Now began the adventure of getting supplies.

6
Trout – We Want Them!

We had a list of what we needed to get before leaving that primarily involved cooking, catching and eating food. We hoped to catch much of our food in the form of Titicaca's famous trucha, and I had brought along a circular plastic fishing rig that I had used successfully in other kayak trips. You carry a big spool of fishing line on your lap with the fishing line trolling behind your boat as you paddle. It fits underneath the spray-skirt, the covering that fits on the kayak to keep water out. If you get a bite, the spool hits the underside of the spray-skirt, which keeps it from flying out. Then you reel it in like a yoyo, hopefully with a nice big trucha on the other end. I had brought some hooks, lures and fishing line, but I hoped to ask the local fishermen what their methods were for catching fish. I soon learned that people don't fish with line and hook, but with nets. I was also surprised to hear that hardly anyone fishes

Titicaca fishing boat

along the shore but rather out of brightly painted wooden boats, which I soon noticed scattered around the lake.

Intent in trying our own time-tested method, we still needed a few important fishing supplies to make our rigs work – most importantly, weights to keep the lures low in the water. We found no fishing supplies in town, so Justin came up with an ingenious system. There were little tourist shops around Copacabana selling blankets, instruments, shirts and little Incan-inspired trinkets made from wood and clay. These little statues came in many forms and were representations of figurines found throughout the Incan empire and their ruins. These were in many of the tourist shops, and they came in different sizes. His idea was to attach a small one to our line to make it heavier, allowing the hook to remain low in the water. I loved this idea as the figurines gave fishing a certain amount of cultural weight to the proceedings! My lure was a puma, which was the symbol of Lake Titicaca and, in fact, the word "Titicaca" translates as "grey puma" in Aymara. I was bound to catch something with that powerful totem. On the other hand, were we supposed to use these sacred figurines to lure a fish into our frying pan? Was this sacrilege? I hoped not.

7
Treasure Hunting

Next on the list of necessities was food. We purchased a good supply of veggies (potato, tomatoes, peppers, cucumbers, onions and garlic), cheese, spices, oil, chocolates and water in the many stores scattered around the central part of town. We counted on catching the *trucha* for the bulk of our protein. I also brought along assorted power bars from home. On previous trips I had learned one could basically survive on these if needed.

For example, on a kayak trip to Malaysia, a friend and I had survived off some green energy food bars for three straight days, eating nothing else as we were uninformed about access to markets…there were none! Although these bars were not the most attractive food item for our palettes (we called them "shit bars"), we appreciated the fact that they kept us from starving and gave us enough energy for our daylong paddles.

Supplies we still needed for our voyage to the islands of Titicaca were kerosene for our backpacking stove as firewood was not plentiful around the lake, and a frying pan and spatula for the trout. Finding the spatula became quite an undertaking. We wandered around all of the little outdoor "knickknack" stores that sold socks, lighters, radios and yogurt looking for what we called "a piece of metal to turn over stuff." The shopkeepers were usually women in colorful hand-made dresses called *polleras* with black bowler hats stylishly pinned to their hair. These stylish hats have been worn by women since the 1920s when the British railway engineers who built the Bolivian railroad system wore them. The women have taken to their sophisticated look ever since. These women were always helpful stating that although they didn't have one, they knew where we could find one.

"Just walk down the way and around the corner."

"*Allí no más*," they all said.

After looping the market place numerous times, we understood that they were just giving us the run-around and probably having a good laugh as well. We went from one sidewalk stand to the next and were told to try "so and so" down the street. This literally lasted for an hour. All we wanted was a simple spatula, people!

Finally hidden underneath some brillo pads, like a gold nugget in a stream, we found a shiny, wonderful – perhaps the best one of its kind – spatula. The only spatula for sale in the town, and we had it...sweet victory!!! We held it up in the air like a trophy, shouting "Spatula, Spatula" and, because of the altitude sickness or mental illness, we kept jumping around with our Incan treasure. We felt this was a good omen for our trip.

Getting the kerosene was another major project. One hour became two hours as we went not from stand to stand or store to store, but from house to house. Somewhere in this town there was a house, colored brown, orange or yellow depending on whom you asked, connected to a garage where you could buy kerosene. We walked down alleys and streets, peeked over fences, walked up stairways, asked and asked, and we could NOT find *"el hombre"* with the kerosene. Was there such a man? It started to seem like a myth, the el Dorado of Lake Titicaca. We really needed the fuel, or we couldn't cook. Just when we had about given up, of course, a young girl called to us from down the street and asked if we were looking for something, and we replied, "Yes, we are looking for kerosene!"

She answered, "Oh, that's my father. Come on in."

We left her house as proud as if we had just passed the bar exam. With two soda bottles filled with kerosene, we were ready to depart.

Stairway to kerosene

8
The Last Meal

Copacabana had taken on a slightly more hippie/hipster feel from when I was there last. Reggae music blared from most restaurants while young male travelers sported beards, dreadlocks, necklaces and colorful Bolivian cloth pants. The women seemed much more simply made up with comfortable jeans, t-shirts and perhaps a look of mild embarrassment for their male counterparts. I must say we were looking no less odd as we headed out to our boats. It's quite cold at 12,800 feet, but we were wearing surfing shorts and brightly colored rash guards, which are often worn while surfing so as not to get a rash on your nipples. They also make for very comfortable paddling shirts. This was the perfect outfit for a day spent paddling many miles, but to the average Bolivian watching us pass by, we looked like circus performers, the "Flying Doofuses," ready for our next trapeze performance.

We decided to have one last "real" meal before leaving and went to one of the many tourist restaurants in town. The menu had the typical tourist fare of eggs, pizza, soups and shakes (not much in the way of typical Bolivian food on the menu – where was the Andean "super grain" *quinoa*?) and, of course, the famous trucha. We skipped the trucha (we would be having this daily, we steadfastly believed) and had veggie omelets, fruits shakes, and coca tea. We liked this particular restaurant immediately, as the cook seemed to be about nine years old and the décor was like somebody's living room. In fact…it *was* someone's living room with kids doing their homework and the family dog scratching her fleas. The cook actually was nine years old! The place was very unassuming, unlike many other restaurants that go out of their way to appear both modern and "native," which is a difficult combination for even the best decorator. The owner of the restaurant (and the father of our young cook) was very friendly. I asked him about sirenas, and he gave us the best story yet.

His cousin took his charango to some sacred rocks overlooking Copacabana. Like others, he used the word *huaca,* and again this *huaca* was not by water (interesting). He placed his charango overnight at the site and in the early morning, when he went to pick it up, he heard the sirena's voice "trapped" inside the charango, singing a hauntingly seductive song. The cousin carried it home with the sirena voice barely audible but still singing. The voice was filled with enchantment, and he was hesitant to bring it into his house where his family could fall under its spell. He decided to stuff the charango inside a wooden box to stifle the enchanting voice, but he could still hear it. He then covered the box with clothes and blankets, but even this couldn't cover up the sirena's voice. He finally had to leave the charango outside, far from his home. The sirena's voice was too strong and powerful, and it scared him. The sirena song finally stopped, but from then on his charango had "special" musical powers. He is now a sought after musician in town. The restaurant owner smiled throughout the story and told us the whereabouts of this place. Although it was very intriguing, since we were looking in particular for sirenas by the water, we decided not to spend the night out looking for his cousin's distant *huaca* as it was some kilometers away in the countryside. Maybe we would check it out after we returned from our paddling trip.

Lake Titicaca

1
Finally on the Water

We got our stuff out of the hotel and loaded all of our belongings into waterproof bags. A crowd of people began watching us as we set up our folding kayak. We extracted the boat from some blue canvas bags, and as they saw us assemble the kayak with its thin frame made of plastic and thin metal poles, they were probably skeptical of its sturdiness. Could it carry Justin, me, plus all of our gear? They watched worriedly as gallons of water, guitars, a stove, multiple food bags and Justin and I in day-glow tight fitting clothes, squashed ourselves into this little boat. We told people that we would be back in two weeks, in case anyone cared, hoping that if we were late, someone would come look for us. I don't think they thought we would survive a day!

Our launch crew in Copacabana

As we were getting ready to leave, some boys about eight or nine years old helped us load up our gear and supplies. I was so impressed with their curiosity even though it worried me a bit to see them flinging themselves into our somewhat fragile-framed boat. Just before leaving, one boy sat down next to me and began pulling on my arm hair as if it was the most normal thing in the world to do. Granted I had more body hair than most Bolivian males (damn my hairy Portuguese genes!), but I wondered what gave them this confidence to interact with strangers. They were also quite interested in our wooden paddles as were some of the adults.

In Copacabana, they had kayaks for rent along the waterfront. They were two-person fiberglass models not made for long trips and with very flimsy paddles. I have been in these exact types of molded kayaks before, even attempting multi-day trips, but found them very uncomfortable with no storage space or legroom. They were functional only for the most short-legged of humans. These kayaks seem to have come from the same mold throughout much of the world.

Once while kayaking in Brazil with a friend, we attempted a long crossing to an island in one of these torturous two-person kayaks. Because there were no spray-skirt covers, our boat began to fill up with water as the day became stormy. We were in the middle of the ocean with the sun setting on the horizon in an increasingly unbalanced kayak. We began to fear capsizing which would result in us swimming several miles back to shore without the boats (probably have to pay for the rotten things), in the dark with who knows what kind of sea monsters lurking beneath. We did make it to a small island only to realize that there was no place to land. We finally ended up crashing onto some rocks and dragging our boats quickly up away from the water to higher ground to sleep in our soaked clothes. We cursed the boats and vowed never to rent this type of kayak again. We also wondered what kind of person would allow people to attempt such a voyage in a rental boat. I could understand them wanting to be rid of us, eaten by sharks with our bones left to bleach on the beach, but they would have also lost their rental kayaks as well. Bad business planning.

Back on the dock by Lake Titicaca, I gave the boys postcards of a beach in Santa Cruz and told them that it was where Justin and I lived and kayaked. I had brought these postcards along to give to people and to remind me of the sirena song that called to me everyday to go out into the Pacific Ocean wilderness. It was important to show them our sacred spot, our *huaca,* which was as impressive as the lake we now found ourselves about to explore. The giant waves amazed the kids as did the lighthouse, which they thought was our home.

2
Out on the Lake

The first few paddle strokes of any kayak trip always leave me feeling giddy. I wanted to shout with joy because now I would be traveling on and living next to water. In a kayak you are free to make your way in the pathless world of water, getting off the much-traveled tourist path. I was so happy to be paddling along the coast of this immense lake (so large I couldn't see the other side) in my own boat with a good friend. We could stop at any time and explore places inaccessible to foot travel that most people would never see. The pace is slow in a kayak, so not only do you get to enjoy every inch of the coastline, but there is also time to enjoy the water's textures and colors which change by the hour or sometimes by the minute.

Just ahead – Isla del Sol

Kayaking gives humans such an intimate relationship with water. Each curve of the water is felt and adjustments are constantly made, much like dancing with a partner while trying to avoid steeping on his or her toes. I always notice that when I pay attention to the water's movements, I move with greater ease. The water shows the path of least resistance, due to currents or swell, and it is a joy to be in tune with this. I become connected with something so much greater than myself, and the small container of myself cracks open. I feel all parts of my body, legs, arms, back and mind tuning in with the fluidity of water travel. When I am paddling and not looking at the water patterns, I find myself in a sense still on land, thinking land thoughts (job, bills, baseball). As soon as I take notice of the water and what it is doing, I am able to push all of my worries and hang-ups to another part of my brain where I don't have to hear them for a while. In my kayak I am as uncomplicated as I ever am.

In the 1980s when I first kayaked along the California coast, paddling my homemade kayak, I would wear nothing but a swimsuit and a spray-skirt even in the winter months with fifty-degree water. I would laugh and scream out loud as my white-water kayak, not entirely suited for ocean travel, would be so bounced around by the winter surf that I would feel myself merge completely into the rise and fall of the waves. The kayak, completely adapted to these conditions, allowed me to imagine what it is like to be a wave in an endless sea. This was always a helpful reminder and metaphor for the rest of my day, framed by life's challenges.

Kayaking also transcends time. When kayaking the waters around Santa Cruz, I feel as if I am returning to an ancient land where, instead of human presence, I travel among otters, sea lions and sharks (even the dreaded great white shark) of the Monterey Bay with its hollowed-out caves, arches, and vast forests of kelp. Now, in this giant lake, the present world dissolved for me and Justin and it felt as if we could be paddling at any time in history.

The only incongruity in this timeless picture was our modern boats filled with gear, so much so that our legs lay over the tops of our waterproof bags as we paddled. There was not an open inch of space on the boat. As we paddled away from Copacabana, another modern reminder zipped by in the form of giant tourist boats, carrying tourists to the Isla del Sol. Isla del Sol is a very popular day trip for people, so boats whisk out of Copacabana and from Puno, Peru many times a day. These boats take people to the two towns of Yumani and Chalampampa, where people walk along ancient trails to the ruins on either side of the island. Tour books recommend spending the night in these towns because the walk across the island takes all day. The last time I visited Lake Titicaca, we wanted to go to Isla del Sol as well, but the idea of getting on a packed boat after being in a van with six people for five months wasn't attractive. It still isn't.

Isla del Sol has been a pilgrimage site for the people of this region predating the Inca. For hundreds of years, people walked for miles along the Copacabana peninsula without eating, in reverence to the sacredness of the island. One person in La Paz said that, for his ancestors, Isla del Sol was like the Muslims journeying to Mecca. It made sense to take our time on the journey and to give the surroundings the respect they deserved. We found ourselves in a sacred land that we really didn't know much about, and it felt important to tread lightly and keep our eyes and hearts open to the many secrets of the area.

3
Rugged Coastline

One of the real surprises of the trip was the beauty of the coastline. As we were traveling during the mostly dry Andean winter, the altiplanos' desolate browns and yellows were in stark contrast to the snowcapped *Cordillera Real* that bordered it. These mountains stretch for about 100 miles along the northeastern edge of the altiplano of Bolivia. As we lost sight of the buildings and roads of Copacabana, the geography along the lakeshore quickly changed to craggy limestone rocks and ragged cliff edges. High above this was the visually interesting and structurally magnificent agricultural terracing that literally covers every exposed surface of the landscape as far as the eye can see. These terraces, which look like the world's most extensive stadium seating, are used to control land degradation. The small rocks that border the steep terraces give way to flattened earth where water is allowed to sink into the soil. It's easy to envision the region as being the breadbasket for corn, which it historically was during the reign of the

A sirena cave?

Inca. Now these terraces appear dried up with just the occasional cultivated field.

As we paddled leisurely down the coast, we also encountered small caves and arches, which were a complete and welcome surprise. For a kayaker, caves and arches allow for access to areas not open to foot travelers. Upon entering a water cave, it feels as if one is entering a Jules Verne novel or a Greek myth where the mystical and fantastic can happen. The sounds of the water bashing against rocks amplify the magical possibilities…sirenas? We poked our boats into every approachable cave and peeked inside with quiet anticipation. Most of the caves were too small to explore very far, and the sharp edges of the entrances threatened our cloth skin boat, but we hoped to find bigger ones in which we could lose ourselves.

The water in lake Titicaca is incredibly clear and combined with the dry landscape has been described as Mediterranean-looking. Plunged into this clarity were submerged rocks, fallen from the rocky cliffs above. Sometimes while getting into the meditative rhythm of paddling and looking at the strange rocky shapes underwater, I would imagine that they were sirena tails. I do this while paddling at home as well, but I imagine great white shark fins instead, which does not conjure up as much joy as a mermaid fin does. There is nothing like imagining you have an eighteen-foot great white shark underneath you to turn a pleasant day's paddle into a horror film. We put our fishing lines out for the first time hoping to have fresh trucha for dinner. The trip was off to an incredible start.

Thankfully, we didn't seem to feel any of the effects of altitude sickness while paddling, which had been a concern to us. It was a physical activity like walking, but for some reason it did not affect our bodies in the same way. We paddled for a couple of hours until we came across our first sandy beach, which looked like an ideal place to take a rest and to redistribute our gear. We now knew what adjustments were necessary to make paddling more comfortable.

We had not caught any fish, not even a bite for that matter, which was a bit of a disappointment. But we were so happy with the beautiful and perfect conditions of the first two hours of the trip that we jumped out of the kayaks just beaming. The weather was ideal, with a light breeze to mask the heat generated by our exertion. On the beach it was warm enough to take off the paddling clothes and sunbathe for a bit. Before arriving here, we had both assumed we would be fully clothed for most of the trip as we predicted cold winds bombarding us throughout the day. Quite the opposite occurred. The conditions were ideal for paddling. Most long-distance kayak trips I have been on have been quite hot (Belize, Costa Rica, Malaysia, Brazil) or cold such as in my hometown of Santa Cruz where it can be freezing with the fog and winter storms. Titicaca was just right.

After a snack of the omnipresent power bars, we brought out a map to plan where we would camp that night. Others had made this kayak trip before us, and they had listed where they had camped on their travel blogs. But we decided early on to base our campsite where we felt sirenas would most likely make an appearance, places with caves or exposed rocks that "looked" like potential *huacas*. The map we were using only provided the most basic outline of the area we were paddling, although in La Paz we had made efforts to find more detailed ones.

We had spent a good chunk of our time in La Paz looking for a topographic or nautical map following any leads given to us. There was a military office that supposedly could provide us with good charts, but South American military departments (we've seen too many Hollywood movies) were not an attractive excursion for us, so we settled for looking for the ultimate tourist map. We were hoping to find the definitive map, something along the lines of "The Ultimate Comprehensive Map of the Magical Islands of Lake Titicaca." Unfortunately, such a map does not exist. We settled for a very basic map made for school children, which at least gave us an idea of the islands' shapes, and enough information to find general locations of little bays that might be suitable for camping. Now looking at this little children's map while actually being on the lake, we realized how unreliable the map was for distinguishing what beaches would actually be good for camping.

4
First Camp

After relaxing on the beach, we rearranged the kayak to better fit our bodies. Our boat was filled with quite a bit of baggage with awkward shapes like plastic gallons of water, frying pans, a spatula, all of which found ways of jabbing our backs or legs. Justin is a little taller than me, a bit over six feet, and it took some time for him to arrange his thin frame in a comfortable position. By the end of the trip, it took us both about twenty minutes to get packed into our boat, but at the beginning it took much longer.

Folding travel boats are wonderful because you can take a boat anywhere on the planet. They come in travel bags, and after about thirty minutes of putting the frame together and slipping on the boat's outer skin (ours was made of rubber and waterproof UV resistant polyester called Hypalon) you are ready to go anywhere. There are limitations away from the water. My kayaks at home are made of plastic or fiberglass and can be dragged up the beach with all the equipment still inside. Folding boats made from more fragile materials need to be unloaded before being brought up the beach and reloaded upon leaving again, or the frames will bend under the strain of so much weight. We were forever trying to find the most efficient method of loading and unloading our boat. At first we looked and felt like slapstick comedians, smacking each other in the head with poles and tripping over waterproof stuff-sacks.

We always loaded the boat at the water edge so we wouldn't have to drag the boat very far, leaving just enough room in the boat to slide in our skinny butts. Justin would usually squash himself in first at the front of the boat, making sure to have water and fishing equipment on his lap for easy access. This usually meant a few minutes of fish hook removal from spray-skirt, seat cushion or thigh. Then we would undoubtedly remember that we had forgotten something vital like the camera, sunscreen, chapstick or water bottle, and we would have to fish it out of one of our many dry bags. With Justin finally packed into the boat, I would try to swivel the

How do we fit in here?

front of the boat around so that it was floating and pointed away from the beach. Now timing was everything. I had to jump into the boat while simultaneously pushing the boat off the shore. If done correctly, by the time I was seated, we would be free of land and floating with both paddles in the water. If the timing was wrong, a number of things could occur. I could fall in the water drenching myself in the cold water, or I could accidentally club Justin in the back of his head with the paddle (which was funny to me), or worst of all, I wouldn't be able to turn the boat in time, and the water would push the boat sideways to the beach where it would dig into the dry sand like a beached whale. Then we would both have to get out of the kayak with fishhook lodged in thigh again, and try the whole sequence again. Rinse and repeat!

After a successful water entry, Justin and I continued our adventure and headed for a small island in front of a town called Titicachi, along the Copacabana peninsula. We had started a bit late, due to the interest in our boats and gear in Copacabana, so by the time we got near the island, the sun was setting. As we approached, we could not find a place to land or find any sign of a beach on which to camp. We passed to the other side of the island that faced Titicachi, where we encountered a woman and man fishing with a net in their little rowboat. They were pulling in their net as we passed, and we greeted them with the trusty greeting *"hola,"* which they very kindly reciprocated. We asked them about their fishing luck, and they solemnly proclaimed *"Malo."* We told them we had little luck as well. The man then asked where we were going to camp, assuming correctly that we would be doing so since the sun was setting and the temperature was plummeting. I liked the fact that he assumed we would be camping rather then looking for lodging in the town, as it meant that camping on the beaches here, even if close to towns, was acceptable. He said we could camp at the next point on the tiny island. We could not see "the point," because this side of the island was surrounded by the tall aquatic *totora* reeds which line much of Lake Titicaca. These are the same reeds from which boats called *balsas* have been made for hundreds of years. *Balsas* were made famous in the trips made by Thor Heyerdahl in his re-creation voyage across the Pacific recounted in the book "Kon Tiki."

Totora reeds

Heyerdahl believed that ancient people of this region made ocean-going vessels which followed the currents across the Pacific, and that these people had perhaps traded with inhabitants of the

Pacific Islands, possibly even colonizing some of these islands. I had read these books as a kid, and they had been a huge inspiration for my dreams of water exploration. These totora boats were still occasionally made on the lake, but because they became waterlogged within six months, the faster and longer lasting wooden boats are now the boats of choice. Today most of the totora reed boats seen on the lake are made for tourist trips or for "re-creation" voyages that are still being made every year across the Pacific Ocean following in Thor Heyerdahl's path.

We plowed through the totora reeds, realizing after the damage was already done that perhaps he meant for us to park our boat to the side of the reeds and carry our equipment to the camp. We hoped there was no permanent damage to the reeds which were now flattened by our clumsy navigating. Acting respectfully is a courtesy I always take seriously everywhere I travel (and at home for that matter) because of the unfortunate stereotype of the ugly "American tourist" that I have no desire to substantiate. We noticed anti-American slogans on many walls around La Paz due largely to our government's unpopular decision to aid in the destruction of coca farms (War on Drugs) that are culturally so important to Bolivia. We wanted to make sure any damage we caused was minimal.

After butchering our way through the reeds to our campsite, we realized how cold it had gotten as the sun sank below the hills surrounding us. It was the kind of wet cold where one's hands can't get warm enough, and they hurt. When paddling a kayak, fingers are curved to fit the shaft of the paddle, and when one finally lets go it takes a while for the hand to break out of this mold. With iced hands it takes even longer for a clump of fingers to become useful appendages.

It took a good fifteen minutes to get all of the gear out of our boat, and as it was getting colder by the second, we set up camp as quickly as possible. Because this was our first night camping, everything was new, so a camping routine had not yet been established. One thing was certain: we would have to arrive at campsites before the sun set from now on. We set up the tents first and stashed all of our multi-colored bags away in an attempt not to

Our messy first campsite

create a circuslike eyesore, as we were in direct view of the little village across the water. We had each brought our own tents so that we could fart to our hearts' content and read all night if insomnia set in. Oh, the unfortunate realities of the middle-aged sleeping body! I remember when I used to share a tent on all my adventures, but now the possibility of my own space seemed a luxury worth lugging another tent around for, while also being respectful and kind to the olfactory space of my travel partner.

Once our gear was put away, we had a short amount of time to create a dinner. As we had not caught one of the famous truchas, we were stuck with potatoes garnished with cheese and spices, a bit meager, yet sounding marvelous. We had a little backpacking stove and with the sought-after spatula, we were ready to go. We had all of our warm clothes on and waited for the meal to cook itself. It became clear from the start that Justin would be the main cook and I the official cutter of ingredients.

These camping arrangements usually make themselves clear at the beginning of a trip when the strengths and weaknesses of a person are out in the open. I am not much of a cook; I don't have the imagination or the patience for it. My favorite recipe in college was the giant pancake. Why bother making a whole bunch of pancakes when you can put all of the batter in one skillet-filling piece of dough. I would eat the enormous pancake, usually burnt on the outside and somewhat raw in the middle as I rode my bike to campus. So simple and packed with starch...the perfect breakfast.

It was obvious from the first bite of dinner that first night that Justin had the necessary skills. What seemed like a sparse meal had become a wonderful and tasty mix of garlic and oregano, pepper and potato. Now with bellies full of good food and freezing hands thawed back to normal, we topped off a wonderful night with... drum roll please... chocolate for dessert, perfect!!

As we sat contentedly digesting our dinner and resting our tired arms, we enjoyed the spectacular view of the small Andean village that lay in front of us while listening to the sounds of mules, cows, goats and llamas. Over this, floating like a beautiful mist, we heard the sound of the *kena,* a notch-holed flute made from bamboo (or bone), which often accompanies the *zampoña* panpipe in Andean ensembles. The scene of this nighttime concert was exquisite. Ancient terraced hills, green with *romero* plants, beans, potatoes, *oka* and quinoa, bordered with little homes made of earth and hatch. A shoreline fringed with totora reeds overlooking a gorgeous section of starlit Lake Titicaca as the classical sound of the Andes, the *kena* flute, played over everything. It felt like an advertisement for the Bolivian tourist board, but it was real. It was a community behaving as it always does, without the heavy handedness of pageantry created for tourists. I had seen this before while traveling in the Amazon where certain river villages behaved in "Disneyesque" interpretations of Amazonian River life. After tourists on their excursion boats left, the villagers put away their feather necklaces, loincloths and ochre paint, put on their t-shirts advertising their favorite Brazilian soccer team and listened to Pink Floyd music.

5
Sirenando

But our night was not over. Now was the time for our first attempt at what we began to term *"sirenando,"* the active search for places where sirenas would be enticed to come and play our instruments. We were on an island with high exposed craggy rocks, and we camped at a point on the island where these were accessible. We headed over to a rocky area to look for our own individual spots that seemed like possible magical spots or *huacas*: a place that would be welcoming for a sirena. This reminded me somewhat of placing the cookie plate for Santa Claus with my son. What is the perfect spot for Santa Claus, and what kind of cookies would he eat? Oatmeal, chocolate chip, peanut butter...we wouldn't want to tick him off. Like my son must have felt with the coming of Santa Claus, I was a bit nervous and filled with real excitement with the possibilities of sirenando.

After some scrambling around on the rocks, I found a little flat rock overlooking the water. With the moon lighting the water's surface with shimmery diamonds, it looked like an exquisite little jazz club stage awaiting the night's artist. Justin went to another spot, far enough away that we could have our own time to commune with the surroundings. I sat down on my rock stage, opened up the charango case, took out my charango and began to tune it. As it was new, and as the strings were also quite new, it required some retuning.

I was so happy to have chosen this charango for its nice warm sound and also because it fit just perfectly over my chest as I played it. Charangos in general have a very rounded back that can make them move around a bit while playing them. This charango snuggled right in. I sat and began to play, improvising on musical themes that I often played at home to relax. After some loosening up, getting my fingers warmer, I began to create some new music influenced by this unique environment. I opened myself up to the creative muse of the lake.

This proved easy to do because not only was I on an emotional rush from my first day out on the lake, but the surroundings were incredibly evocative. The half-full moon in the sky was reflecting on the water and the light refractions shimmered and danced. Water patterns are endlessly beautiful, intriguing, mystical and artistic to me. I am such a sucker for them. If I ever see a photograph or painting of water, I am drawn to it like a magnet and want to own it. My wife is very used to this behavior and keeps me moving along, lest we have wall-to-wall water pictures and no college fund for the kids.

I concentrated all my attention on the patterns made from water and moonlight, and soon a distinctive rhythm and melody came out. My compositions are usually quite mellow, a release from the chaos of the day, but here on top of this rock looking down on the water, I began to play with more percussive intensity. I, for some reason, wasn't feeling mellow at all, lulled by the peaceful lapping waters. Instead, I was completely awake as if in the anticipatory excitement of a first date. This was a moment that I had been envisioning for a long time, and I was happily surprised to be feeling in tune with my creative side so early in the trip.

A sirenando *ledge*

After playing for a while and feeling tired, I placed my charango on a flat rock overlooking the water. I had read in Thomas Turino's article that there was some ceremony involved in the presenting of the charango to the sirenas, but I very much wanted the ritual aspect of the trip to be as organic as possible, and for our actions and offerings to be from our own intuitiveness. I knew that you are supposed to leave the charango out overnight, but should I leave it out in the open, or enclosed in its case? Should I leave an offering...and what should that be? I also felt nervous about leaving my charango out in the elements without its case. Maybe there were animals around that would chew on it!

I decided to leave the charango in the case but with the case open. If a sirena were to come, then she would not have to physically open up the case, but the charango would still be more or less protected from the elements and curious creatures. I was assuming that when the water spirit came, it would be a she, as a merman seems more imposing. Just the thought gave me disturbing images of a large muscular merman thrashing my charango to a watery version of heavy metal. Although I suppose there would be no reason a mermaid wouldn't also play heavy metal music, I was assuming the sirena would have more melodic musical tastes. I began to wonder how the sirena would physcially play the charango? Would she place it on her lap and play a song, or just pluck the strings a few times and then go back into the water?

This was all new territory for someone who had never seen a sirena before. Even more amazing was to realize that these ideas were even coming to my head and that Justin was going along with this as well, without laughing, or at least not outwardly! Justin, in fact, seemed to be as entranced by the area as I was as he continued his nighttime concert after I had headed back to camp, exhausted by the day's adventures. Just this morning we had been inside a hotel filled with tourists, televisions and pizzas, and now we were on an island by ourselves with stars, guitars, and hopefully sirenas. What an amazing planet we live on! With the possibilities of sirenas in my head, I remembered another time I had fallen into the realm of water spirits.

When I was twenty-one years old, I had the amazing opportunity to join a research trip to study the Amazon pink river dolphin, with the Brazilian biologist Vera de Silva of INPA, the Amazon Research Institute. We traveled the length of the Amazon River in a research boat filled with scientists studying a wide range of subjects concerning the immense watershed of the Amazon River Basin. Vera and I were stationed on top of the boat where we sat all day counting dolphins, watching these remarkable creatures, observing behavior, and getting extremely tan. Their pink coloring, unique long beaks and melon-shaped head, gave them an otherworldly, entrancing look. As they swam beneath the blue sky surrounded by the green forest and brown river, it often felt as if I had been dropped into a surrealist painting or a Dr. Seuss cartoon.

It is no wonder that there are endless stories of the pink dolphins being entrancing and seductive, the Amazonian mermaid. According to local knowledge, these dolphin creatures could be male or female, disguising themselves as human, with hats to cover up their blowhole. It was believed by some that deformed babies were a result of liaisons between humans and dolphins. I was told by someone from a village along the river to be careful not to walk by the river at night on a full moon, as I would be seduced and drawn to the depths of the river by a *boto* (dolphin) to their underwater kingdom, never to be seen again. As a young, impressionable man of twenty-one, and game for anything, the proposition sounded adventurous and somewhat attractive.

As I jumped into my sleeping bag, hearing Justin playing softly and so enchantingly, I could not believe that his musical notes wouldn't attract the sirenas of Lake Titicaca to our little camping spot. As I closed my eyes and entered dreamland, I was so proud of us. Two guys who didn't really know each other that well, open to the possibility of magic in the surroundings, and we were facing everything in our new adventure with a good sense of humor. The idea of searching for mermaid songs in Lake Titicaca made us laugh out loud at just the thought of it. This was the kind of unrestrictive laughter and joy we both remembered having in childhood, as we searched for dragons or imagined ourselves as professional baseball players in the World Series. Abandonment of mental restrictions is good for the soul, though not a normal activity in our daily lives, or sadly, in most peoples lives at all. "Honey, I'm off to listen to the Earth sing to me" is not heard as often as it probably should be. "Honey I'm off to buy a new electrical gadget" is unfortunately, much more common.

6
Cold Night

I woke up a few times in the night to drink water, as one can get quite thirsty with the *soroche* (altitude sickness). The wind had picked up quite a bit, and I became worried that my charango might have blown off the cliff. I had wrongly assumed that the winds would be strongest during the day and calm in the morning and night. Most of the other kayaking trips I had been on in the past had followed this pattern, so I assumed we would always try to get an early morning paddle to avoid strong winds. So far the paddling had been very calm in the day, and the wind was strong at night. The picture of my charango nose-diving into the lake played through my mind as I tried to stay warm in my sleeping bag.

I sadly realized that my sleeping bag was not as warm as it needed to be, and began experimenting with clothing options. Clothes on or clothes off? That was the question. Is it warmer to be naked in a sleeping bag, or with layers of warm clothes on? Logically fully clothed made sense, but it seems like I am always warmer without clothes on, so I decided to try this option first. The idea of putting my clothes back on and walking in the wind to check on the charango was too much; I was just too tired, and I didn't want to interrupt the sirena creating other worldly musical masterpieces on my charango.

Dreamily, I thought of my water home in Santa Cruz and the distinctive sounds of the Monterey Bay. The haunting heartbeat of the "one-mile" buoy that I can hear in my bedroom every night, and the roar of the waves during a winter storm. I realized that the ocean has been a constant soundtrack for much of my life. Waves and seagulls were in the background when I asked Gwynne to marry me, and at our wedding as well. These sounds are as familiar to me as my own breathing. As I tried to sleep, I imagined myself back in this ocean realm, my home, surrounded by its unique beauty, and its own sirens of the deep.

In Monterey Bay, there are numerous creatures that interact with humans in the water. I have had sea otters throw shellfish onto my kayak; I have swum side by side with harbor seals with huge beautiful eyes and have played chase with dolphins for over an hour. I have had immense grey whales slide within feet of my kayak and have had sea lions bark at me as I surfed by their rocks. These interactions – an underwater world of mysteries – seem like forms of communication that are alluring to me. I often find myself surprisingly daydreaming about what I would do if one of these sea creatures motioned for me to follow it underwater, to its special world. Would I go? If a seal said, "Hey buddy, come and check out our fantastic world underwater," would I take the plunge? I remember hearing about Jacques Cousteau coming across a circle of dolphins gathered together, fins pointed down and snouts pointed up, as if they were standing in a meeting. They dispersed when they saw him, but not before he was able to see perhaps a world of communication between sea creatures much "deeper" than we have previous thought. The water world is incredibly seductive to me.

While living in Costa Rica, when the ocean was calm enough, I would often lie face down in the watery darkness, letting the waves roll over me. As I floated with just my legs lightly touching the sand below, I would be lulled into a sort of meditative state. After doing this for a while, I often felt that I could almost forget to breathe as I became perfectly in tune with the rhythms of the waves and the warm embrace of the tropical surf. If it wasn't for the fact that after a while my body got too cold, I often wondered if this could have actually happened. These late night swims were truly hypnotizing and a little unsettling. I was almost too comfortable and calm in the water.

7
First Morning

I woke up to a frosty morning, pulled myself out of my sleeping bag, put on all my warm clothes and headed over to the point of rocks where our instruments were. The sun hadn't appeared yet, but it was light enough to see where I was going as I walked along the shoreline and came to our "sirenando" spot. Thankfully the charango and guitar were still there, but my adrenaline now surged with a different question? How would my charango sound? The first thing I noticed was that the charango was totally wet. As I had left the case open overnight, the morning frost had soaked my instrument. I had not thought of this and hoped I did not destroy my instrument on our first night of camping.

I took out the charango, shook off some of the water droplets and was ready for my first field test of magical charangos. I had been waiting for this moment for many years, and my mind was open to anything. Had a sirena come in the night to compose on my charango? Were there magical vibrations in this piece of wood and string? I strummed…nothing happened…I strummed again, and even though I did not exactly know what I was supposed to hear, I felt that I was not feeling anything except the rush of anticipation. I did, however, notice that the strings were more or less in tune with one another. This was odd because the charango had been out all night exposed to high winds and a dewy frosty morning, which would usually affect the elasticity of the strings. I played the charango with more respect now. This was not overwhelming evidence of having a sirena experience but intriguing all the same.

Justin wandered over and looked at me as if to say, "Well, did the sirena visit last night?" with just the right mixture of adult nonchalance and childlike anticipation. I showed him the charango and played a bit, and he felt it sounded surprisingly in tune as well. His guitar was even more soaked as he did not leave it on or in his cloth case, but with a few tweaks it was also surprisingly not too out of tune. We played for a while on the warm rocks in the welcome morning sun and then headed back to the campsite for breakfast. It was true that the instruments had more or less stayed in tune, but neither one of us felt we had a "sirenando" experience. If asked, I am sure we would have had a difficult time articulating exactly what we were expecting to happen, but this did not seem to be it...yet.

On the way back to camp, we met the fisherman whom we had seen the night before in his boat with his wife. He had rowed over from the town of Titicachi. The night before we had asked him if we could buy fish in his town, as our fishing attempts had failed. He said he would come by in the morning and bring us some. It felt a bit strange to ask for fish when we had our own fishing supplies, but he himself had told us the fishing had not gone well for him, either. In fact, purchasing or trading for food is a wonderful way to meet local people while traveling. My thin body type, leaning towards gaunt depending on whatever intestinal problem I might be having, gives me a pathetic look that has often led people to take pity on me.

Some years ago in Cuba, where my wife and I were working as children's performers, we had to ride our cheap Chinese bikes everywhere on little or no food. We were sharing a house with Cubans, living off their meager ration cards and some black market items we were able to purchase. Before too long, I had gotten quite skinny and people who hardly even knew me began bringing me anything to put some meat on my bones. Supplies were often so low that all they could offer me was a cigar and glass of rum (generous helpings of these staples were still available with their ration cards) which, in retrospect, may not have helped me gain any weight but showed concern none-the-less. I guess that in their minds, I just wasn't making it on my own. A skinny white boy, obviously in need of some help. This is what we must have looked like drifting into the little cove on Lake Titicaca the previous evening asking for fish – pathetic foreigners in need of aid.

The man from Titicachi kindly asked how our night was. I mentioned the glorious *kena* music that drifted over to us in the night, and he nonchalantly said that it was he who was playing. My wife is a wonderful kena player, so I know how they can sound, but he really had something distinctive to his talent, a John Coltrane on *kena*. I told him that he had made our first night on the lake perfect, and mentioned our plans to try and find places to entice sirenas to play our stringed instruments so that we could hear her music. It was freeing to feel no embarrassment at all in saying this! As normal as asking if the San Francisco Giants had won a ballgame back home. He smiled and said that people for generations have done so and that they had put their instruments (his *kena* flute included) by some rocks at a point on the other side of the small island on which we were camped. I showed him where we had placed our instruments, and shared how I felt that my charango had stayed in tune even when wet. He smiled and nodded sagely, with no smugness or sign of doubt or cynicism. Judging from his musical abilities, it was apparent he appreciated the power in one's surroundings to inspire artistic creation. I thought of the music he played enveloping the small island where we had camped, and how it was, in fact, a "siren" song that captured our hearts. It is a wonderful feeling to talk about matters of the heart to other men, a thing that doesn't happen nearly often enough.

 He also told us that he unfortunately did not have any fish for us and then detonated the "bomb shell' statement that would affect us for the rest of the trip: "No Hay Trucha." The world-famous Lake Titicaca trout had been over-fished (for tourist consumption, no less) and the trucha was rarely caught anymore. He said fishermen had caught all of the juvenile fish before they had reached sexual maturity, causing a rapid decline in the trucha population. He had a very matter-of-fact expression that belied the sadness of the statement. We later learned that the trucha had been, in fact, introduced in the 1930's and was not a native fish. What a letdown! We had imagined fresh fish with limes and garlic every night. Also disheartening was the fact that we were going to be very low on food now, especially protein. I didn't want to have another experiment on how the human body reacts to eating a pure green/protein bar diet.

 With trucha seemingly out of the picture, we were going to have to try our best at catching any aquatic life at all (sirenas notwithstanding). After all, people were out fishing for something. We also realized we would be more dependent on buying food from the villages we passed, and the prospect of eating tinned sardines on the shores of Titicaca was disheartening. Over-fishing was becoming a common thread in my travels of different waters of the world. Even my home of Santa Cruz has seen local populations of fish plummet and livelihoods of the fishermen become increasingly difficult if not impossible. Sad.

This *kena*-playing fisherman seemed (unfortunately I can not recall his name, as I would love to add his name to my list of favorite musicians) to be a sort of defacto mayor of the small village of Titicachi. He asked how our night was on "their" island, which we simultaneously replied in our immaculate spanglish "Super bueno!!" He informed us that he wanted to create a big totora reed boat which could carry tourists out on this little alcove of the lake. He dreamed of a small restaurant that would, ironically, serve trucha.

I mentioned a man who was written about in our guidebook, Señor Quispe, who supposedly had lots of stories about the folklore of the area and who lived in the next village on the peninsula, and it was as if I had stepped on his toes with cleats. I got the feeling that Señor Quispe had stolen some of the fire away from our fisherman friend's position as potential leader and tourist liaison of the area. I immediately dropped the subject and we shook hands and thanked him for coming out to talk with us.

After breaking down camp and loading the boats, we were ready to head out to our next section along the lake. We hoped to make it as far as Yampupata, the village closest to the Isla del Sol, or perhaps even make it to the island itself. We didn't want to tell our new friend, but we were indeed going to try to visit the infamous Señor Quispe, written about in our guidebook as the "man to see" in these parts for stories and information on the region.

8
The Man

We slid through the totora reeds and looked back at our first campsite for the last time, then paddled around the corner for our next adventure. Throwing our fishing lines in the water, we decided to tempt fate and try our luck at catching something to eat along the way. Our trawling method was either ingenuous or pathetic. We had the fishing line attached to a hook weighted by the wooden Incan idols. Attached to the hook were some florescent green rubber worms that tangled brightly behind us as we paddled. Yum!

The weather conditions again created perfect paddling. A light breeze cooled off our bodies, as we paddled our 450-pound load across the smooth lake. It was effortless; the sun was out and the landscape was a spectacular vista of blue lake, snowcapped mountains and brown earth. We passed more caves and rocky beaches that looked ideal for sirenas to sun themselves. Justin and I were getting to know each other. We talked about things that in our hurried day-to-day lives we usually wouldn't find time to talk about.

Perfect paddling conditions

It felt great, and I realized how much I missed having an adventure friend. It's not just the adventure, it is also the time to spend talking about how crazy, exhausting, sad, happy and ultimately wonderful life can be. Find a friend, have an adventure, and the necessary thoughts and topics of interest will come out; catharsis through adventure. Move those bones, move the mind!

We knew that around the next point was the town of Sicuani, the home of Señor Quispe. Our plan was to paddle over and, hopefully, have lunch with him at the small restaurant he owned. If it seemed like it was worth staying overnight in the town to learn about local customs and folklore from Señor Quispe, we would try to camp there. The great thing about this trip, and most trips I have been on, is that there was no schedule or specific destinations. We had uncovered just enough information to give us a general idea of what was in store for us, with the details being left to fate. So we paddled, talked, didn't catch fish and marveled over the beauty of it all.

Passing around the point, we saw in the cradle of a small bay, the little town of Sicuani, and we paddled up to a gap in between the totora reeds. To one side was a brightly-covered tourist excursion boat tied up to a small dock as well as remnants of a totora raft. The town looked small and deserted, so we headed up onto the main road looking for signs of life. There was a well-worn sign that had Señor Quispe's name somewhat legibly displayed on it (very convenient), so we knew we were in the right place. There still wasn't anyone around, which was odd. We wandered a little ways down the dirt main road that bisected the town, which we were surprised to even see as there were no cars. We finally encountered a person who was working in an agricultural field at the water's edge. We walked down to him and mentioned Señor Quispe. The sign on the road mentioned that he had a restaurant and a tourist agency, so we assumed that this farmer would most likely know him. He smiled at us when we asked him and then went on to speak to us in slurry, strangely metered language. There were pieces of Spanish and, I assumed, Aymara, but there was an odd look to him that made me think that perhaps he was a little bit mad. Of course, we probably looked somewhat the same to him in our bright paddling gear.

He saw the instruments strapped to our boats down at the water's edge and asked (or so we thought) if we were going to record here. Did he mean in his field? We sorted out eventually that some time in the past a well-known Peruvian group had recorded music here. We told him we were not intending to do any recording here at this particular time, intriguing as it seemed, and that we were, in fact, waiting for Señor Quispe's return. He smiled, we smiled, neither of us really understanding what the other was saying. Chickens and ducks conversing.

We walked back towards our boats resigned to the fact that we would not meet this famed man when we came across the only other person wandering about, who identified himself as Señor Quispe's son! He said his father had gone into Copacabana for supplies and would be back later. The boy earnestly answered some of our questions about the region. How many people lived here? (100) Were there any charango players in town? (yes) We also wondered if any foreigners lived in town, and he said there was one "Americano" who lived there sometimes. We asked him what he did, and he said, "He does nothing." I suppose that is probably what people think about a lot of the ex-patriots who are scattered all over the globe. You find them sitting at bars drinking, resting or reading, and wonder what they do when they are not there. I have lived in a few Latin American towns where I saw the same Americans at the local bar every night where they would stay until the bar closed. These men seemed too young to be retired, so I often wondered what they did during the day. Were they land developers waiting for the small town to be "discovered," CIA people – or were they perhaps hiding from some dubious, nefarious past? The locals thought they just were probably lazy and did "nothing."

The young Quispe was also very interested in our kayak. He wanted to know how much gear fit in it, how much did it cost, and was fascinated with the two-sided kayak paddles. I think he probably hoped we would give him one, which unfortunately we couldn't. We asked him if he could help us find something hard, like a piece of wood, to reinforce a backrest that we had broken on the kayak. We went up to his house along the dirt road where he introduced us to his mother, Doña Quispe. We asked her if she had anything that could fix our kayak seat, and though she was nice enough about our request, she smiled and said that she really didn't have anything to spare. I realized as I left their very rudimentary, but entirely efficient home, that whatever they had, they used. There were no extra "scraps" lying around. As we left the house, we passed by a llama owned by the family and asked if it had a name. The boy said it was Juana. Juana the llama, perfect!

We decided to leave town without waiting to see his father, because we wanted to get closer to Isla del Sol that night, and besides, his son had been a great source of information. Back at the boat we shared some power bars with our new young friend (a sorry gift, I know) and he allowed us to take a picture of him in the rotting totora boat that his father had made to lure tourists here, an idea that perhaps hadn't materialized yet. The boy didn't seem to mind one way or the other. We told him to give his father our regards and waved a sincere "adios" to our little guide. Our time with him was worth much more than any tourist kiosk or brochure describing life in the area could have offered.

Our wonderful young guide in Sicuani

9
Passing Through History

Our next destination was the town of Yampupata (Justin's favorite town name), which was the final stop before crossing over to the Isla del Sol. We would spend the night here if there was a nice place to camp on the outskirts of town, and we could get up the next morning to cross over to the island. It felt, in a way, that our adventure would really begin once we were on Isla del Sol, which was coming tantalizingly closer with each stroke of our paddles! Like pilgrims hundreds of years before us, we were following a path to an island of great spiritual significance.

Isla del Sol is one of the most important religious sites in the Andean world. Incans considered it the birthplace of the Sun. The Inca believed Viracocha, the Creator God, rose from the waters of Titicaca and called forth the sun and the moon from a rock on the island. It is also the largest island in Lake Titicaca, 21 km long and 8 km across its widest point.

Isla del Sol was an important religious site even before the arrival of the Inca. The Tiwanaku ruled the Titicaca basin around AD500 and built large shrines on Isla del Sol which are still visible on the island today. After conquering the region in the mid-fifteenth century, the Incan empire built their own shrines and temples, often on top of the Tiwanaku shrines. During this time, the whole Copacabana peninsula, as well as the Isla del Sol and Isla de La Luna, was cleared of its indigenous population and turned into restricted sacred areas for priest astronomers and the people who tended them.

Today, although the ancient structures are in ruins, several thousand Aymara campesinos still follow the traditional lifestyles of the region – fishing, herding llamas and cultivating the Inca agricultural terraces that contour the island's steep slopes. These people whom we were passing in our boats were living in much the same way they had been living for hundreds of years.

10
Yampupata

While paddling in the late afternoon sun, we were getting a little tired, and Justin actually started to feel some uncomfortable tinges in his wrist (tendonitis!), so we decided it was time to find a strand of beach outside of Yampupata to rest ourselves before the freezing wind settled in. Unfortunately, a beach didn't materialize. By the time we pulled up to Yampupata, we realized we would probably have to camp within the towns limits, which we didn't want to do. On the positive side, at least we could probably find a good meal in a local restaurant to fortify ourselves.

We pulled up to the mini-harbor where all the fishing boats were anchored and walked up the beach past some people who took no notice of us. This was comforting, but also strange. In Copacabana and Titichachi our kayak had been an interesting novelty to be investigated, and we were often questioned about our trip. Here it actually felt as if we were being avoided. Because this town was the last stop before heading to Isla del Sol, tourists often arrived here

Looking out of place in Yampupata

looking for boats to take them to the island. Perhaps it was because the locals were fed up with being a stepping-stone to another place that we received such a frosty reception, the Andean cold shoulder! Then again, perhaps it was our appearance. We were in our usual attire of brightly-colored surf rash-guards, surf shorts, sunglasses, wide-brimmed hats and tennis shoes. Not the usual attire for men in these villages. They may have thought, like many elsewhere in South America, that it was inappropriate for men to wear shorts.

I had experienced this during my first job in another country. The job was at INPA, the Amazon research institute in Manaus, Brazil. I had come from the "shorts everyday" environment of the University of California, Santa Barbara, and was thrust into a culture where everyone wore long pants and buttoned-down shirts, even while working with animals in the extremely hot tropical sun. I remember thinking, "Where is the scantily clad world of Samba and carnival?"

As we strolled through Yampupata, it suddenly dawned on us that it was Sunday, which made us not only look weird, but possibly disrespectful to those adhering to certain Christian rituals. As we were quite hungry, we ignored the cool reception and walked further into town looking for food. We found one restaurant advertised in our guidebook, but, of course, it wasn't open. It actually did not look like it had been open for quite a while. It seemed that hard times had met this part of the world since the writing of our guidebook.

As we did not feel entirely welcome in this little town, we decided to tempt fate and make the crossing to the Isla del Sol. Hopefully, we would land there before the sun went down and the serious cold set in. We slipped away in our kayak after asking an older man who was sitting on the beach if he knew anything about sirenas in the lake. He grumpily responded in perhaps Spanish, perhaps Aymara, we couldn't tell, and in the middle of his speech waved us away. Was he going to flip us off next? Strange and unsettling... what did this all mean? Were we that offensive? Was the mention of a siren sacrilegious to some people? It could very well be that in some areas the church still frowned upon such beliefs – God knows this is true in the United States. It was then that I realized I would have to be more tactful in approaching people about sirenas and perhaps ask more mundane questions to help a person feel somewhat more comfortable before asking about my true interests. How's the weather been lately, now tell me where the sirenas are!

Isla del Sol

1
Isla del Sol Arrival

The guidebooks had said Isla del Sol was "a stone's throw away," but as we paddled for half an hour and still had not reached the island's shore, we realized it would have to have been an amazing stone thrower. As the sun began to set, we saw a small beach to the left of the main town of the island, Yumani, and headed for it. We wanted to camp near Yumani so that we could make a short hike there in the morning, eat a good breakfast and buy some more supplies. As the town is on the top of the island, with supposedly breathtaking views, we would also get a clearer sense of what our kayak trip around the island might entail.

We finally arrived (sadly, the sun was already down) at a little rocky beach beneath some high cliffs, with what looked like a small ranch perched a few hundred feet above. We immediately unloaded the kayaks, pulled our boat up the beach and set up camp. It was a repeat of the night before with frozen hands trying their best to be helpful, but working about as well as a foot attached to an arm. Dinner again was simple, but our dessert of chocolate was the perfect remedy for our exhausted bodies. All we could think of was going to bed, but having finally arrived on Isla del Sol, I was also motivated to begin sirenando in earnest. There was an outcropping of rocks at the side of the beach, coal-colored in the twilight. I went to investigate.

After putting on every strip of clothing I owned, I walked over to the rocks with my charango and started to play. This was to become part of a nightly ritual: the creation of a song that originated in the waters in front of me. My idea was to play random chords and rhythms, and hopefully a song would materialize. Again I was surprised that the natural rhythm that came to me was not slow and introspective but a fast, loud, frantic driving rhythm. Again, it probably had something to do with the intensity of this starkly beautiful place and the emotions of finally being on this island of my dreams.

As I sat perched on these rocks playing my charango, overlooking the lake and the mainland that we had just traversed, I was overcome with thankfulness. Isla del Sol was geologically more interesting than I had imagined, and so far the trip was going very well. The magic that I had hoped to feel was there, and I felt in the right "space" for more to come. While continuing to stare at the water, its patterns and rhythms for continued inspiration, I played a series of chords over and over in different combinations until they resembled the beginnings of a song. I felt that if I were true to myself and my heightened emotions, my playing might call the lake spirits to the charango. I would create my own siren's song.

I played until my hands got too cold to make the proper finger movements, and then I decided to look for a perch on which to lay my charango – part two in my sirenando ritual. Again I was confused as to whether I should leave my charango outside of its case, or have it lie in the case with the lid open? Or, should I have the charango on top of the case or perhaps outside and away from the case altogether? Confusing, this sirenando business. I finally decided to leave the charango inside the case with the lid open, as I had on Titichachi, even though the strings would probably get wet as they had the previous evening. Because of the growing wind, I had to position the case so that the wind would not close it, potentially smashing the sirena's fingers! I even positioned the case next to a flat comfortable rock for the sirena's comfort. Just trying to be gentlemanly, you know. It was getting quite cold, so I looked one last time at my instrument, found the position to be fine, and headed back to the campsite.

2
Tides?

Back in the tent I stayed up for a while reading and writing, but had a hard time concentrating. I was actually finally on the friggin' Island of the Sun!!!!! On this little beach with my charango, kayaking with a good friend, I could easily just let my mind enjoy the trip at face value, or I could truly entertain the possibilities of the mystical and allow my imagination to roam in this evocative place uncluttered with cynicism and skepticism. As I tried to sleep, the dramatic surroundings filled my dream world with strange images of ancient cities of gold surrounded by raging rivers of water. Water everywhere...in fact, the water seemed to be right outside my tent....

"WATER!!!" Justin screamed out. I hopped out of my tent and saw that our kayak was in the process of being pulled into the water. Water was pouring into the boat, and in the darkness I could see things floating out of the boat and into the lake. The water line had moved about four feet onto the beach. What the hell was going on! Were there tidal differences in Lake Titicaca? We went into emergency mode. I knew we could not pull the boat onto the beach filled with water because the frame would bend. So grabbing pots, Justin and I began to frantically bail out our boat to make it light enough to carry up the beach. Who knew what we had already lost to the lake. We did this for a while in the dark with the cold wind blowing. We didn't talk, we just kept scooping water out. Eventually, we were able to pull the boat up onto the beach without damaging the frame. As relief set in I suddenly remembered...my charango! Had the tide snatched my charango away?

I ran, I mean sprinted, in the dark towards the rocks where I had placed my charango, cutting my foot on something sharp along the way. It was dark, my foot was bleeding, my adrenaline was pumping and I could not find the charango. I looked and looked in the dark, but couldn't find it – CRAP! I should have at least brought my flashlight. My legs were all jittery as the realization came over me that my charango/*sirena* exploration might be over. But then in a pool of water, I saw a black case. My charango...YES! I grabbed it, pulled it out of the water, and to my surprise the case was soaked but the charango seemed to be all right – wet, but not ruined. I strummed it, and, to my amazement, it was still in tune! I immediately dried it off on my jacket, grabbed the case and ran back to camp. There was still much to do in camp, and I probably should have stayed with Justin and gotten all of our soaked items out of the boat so they could dry overnight, but Justin understood my charango emergency. He too was amazed that it was still in tune. We spent the next hour moving our campsite away from the encroaching tides of Lake Titicaca. I put the charango back in my tent and fell into an exhausted sleep. *Sirenando* would have to wait until the next beach.

3
Yumani

I woke up with the sun and peeked out my tent window to see a now entirely tranquil lake, quite different from the one we experienced the previous night. But still COLD! I stayed in the tent until I could see the sun rise beautifully from behind the Isla de la Luna, which lay in front of us. This was where we were going for the second part of our trip and it looked invitingly small and unpopulated. With the sun up, Justin and I had a simple breakfast of protein bars and some oranges and talked about the previous night's madness. Tides in a lake seemed unlikely, and we realized the difference in water height was probably due to the incredible nighttime winds we had experienced, pushing water across the lake. We would have to be more careful where we camped. We commented on the interesting fact that my charango strings were still in tune, even though they had all gotten wet and then spent the night drying in my tent. This shouldn't happen with wet strings, should it? Perhaps it was the cold weather that preserved

Marvelous views of Yumani

the tensions of the strings. Or something else…sirenas?

We decided to head into Yumani to get some supplies and have some restaurant food. This was the biggest of three towns on the island and was where most of the boats dropped off tourists who came to walk to the ruins on the other side of the island. We headed up the trail towards the town passing the steep terraces that lined the entire island. Unlike many of the terraced fields we had passed on our trip to the island, some terraced fields around the Isla del Sol were under cultivation. The lush green hillsides here are said to be very fertile because they are insulated by the waters of the lake making for higher ground temperatures than the mainland. There are also underground springs which nourish the crops. Isla del Sol was an important producer of sacred *maize* during the Incan empire. Corn is said to grow better on Isla del Sol then any other place in the Titicaca basin. Other important crops grown are potatoes, beans, quinoa and barley. The amount of work that went into the creation and the continued maintenance of these terraced fields is amazing as the slopes on much of the island are very steep.

Fuente del agua

On the way to Yumani we would pass the famous *"Fuente del Agua"* a place where the three springs that nourish the soil and provide fresh water to the islanders meet together in a stone basin.

These springs are believed to have magic power, and drinking from all three sources is supposed to give you good luck. We looked forward to seeing these springs and perhaps drinking from them, although I am always wary about drinking untreated water, even if it is from underground springs. Justin had bought a very expensive filter for our trip, and we also had bottled water from Copacabana. Past experience has made me unwilling to take any unnecessary chances drinking untreated water.

I have had three bouts of the water-born parasite Giardia, which leave its victims with intense cramping, diarrhea and subsequent weight lost. My last bout left me sick for months with symptoms still apparent to this day. I know the exact source of my last encounter with this tiny, yet diabolical beast. I was again kayaking, this time with two Peace Corps friends in Costa Rica as part of a sea turtle education project. We paddled the entire length of the Pacific Ocean side of Costa Rica performing interactive songs and activities about sea turtles. It was a wonderful trip that lasted forty-five days taking us to many small rural towns. On one of the last days, we were offered glasses of lemonade from an elderly lady next to her very rustic home. It looked so inviting and she seemed so sweet and friendly, we said, "yes," and drank with gusto. Later, I walked around to the back of her house and saw that her water source was a small open well looking very unclean, with pigs and chickens roaming freely all around it. Within the week, I was an uncommonly frequent visitor to the restrooms of Costa Rica. On Isla del Sol, relieving oneself turned out to be much more pleasant – transcendent even.

As we left our campsite on this beautiful day, nature called, so I picked a place on the side of a hill behind some shrubs where I had a fantastic view. With the sun shining and a slight, warm breeze caressing my face, I sat and breathed in the pure air at 12,000 feet. I could see the majestic snow-peaked *Cordillera Real* (the Royal Range), the deep blue lake and Isla de la Luna lying serenely in front of me. I felt as if I could have stayed there for the entire morning enjoying the sights. But, alas, we had other things to take care of like getting more water and vegetables in town.

Coming into town we were thrown into the world of tourism–the good, the bad and the ugly. The first place we passed on our arduous hike into town was a beautiful rustic lodge fronted by a gate. We wanted to go inside to see if they had any good information about the history of the island but some friendly local Aymara standing by smiled at us benignly and said that it was *privado* – a private tourist lodge that we couldn't enter. How misguided and perplexing it seemed to physically separate oneself from everyone else in this small beautiful island. Just a little up the hill was the small town that looked entirely beautiful and much more inviting. Why would visitors want to be in an exclusive gated community away from the people and culture they came to visit? This is an all too common reality in international tourism, I'm afraid. We passed their wealthy prison, relishing our freedom.

We ordered a breakfast at a little rustic hostel overlooking the lake. There were two kinds of breakfast offered. The "American" breakfast included bread (which I couldn't eat) – yogurt, jam, coffee or tea and an egg. The "Continental" breakfast was toast (out of luck again), fruit, tea or coffee. Asking for any variations on these combinations produced stern-faced looks, or, at the very least, raised eyebrows on the waitresses. Our requests for refills of tea were met with visible agitation. You get what you get, greedy tourist. This tourist place was filled with travelers, and most seemed to be sitting in complete silence. This would have been fine if they were looking at the utterly incredible view in front of them, but many seemed to be staring at their burning cigarettes. I was assuming most were from Europe (the smoldering intensity), but as they were not talking I couldn't tell. So, all in all, we didn't fit in here as we were talking, smiling, laughing and enjoying the view, sans tobacco. We were probably as odd to them as they were to us. Plus we wanted refills of tea, an Isla del Sol "no-no." It was time to move on.

Moving on meant finding some food for our trip. We needed some basics, especially some fresh veggies and fruit. We figured that Yumani, the biggest town on the island, would have produce from the lush gardens seen on the surrounding terraced fields. Apparently we were wrong. We walked around to all of the little

Justin eating Desayuno Americano *in Yumani*

mini stores selling crackers, toilet paper, candies and water asking if they had vegetables, and the answer was always no. When we asked if they knew where we could find some, they either said no, or worse, they would point to an area higher up on the heart-attack-inducing slope. Onwards we hiked in vain, sweating, panting and gasping for breath, like enormous men on treadmills.

As we searched for the elusive vegetable, we passed by an interesting group of men who were sitting in the shade of a brick wall to keep out of the sun. One gentleman spoke to the group in hushed Aymara, the women sat on the other side of the courtyard in silence. They looked very serious and didn't look at us or notice us as we walked by, just listened intently to the speaker who spoke quietly. We imagined his lecture....

"Please, no vegetables to foreigners, this is of utmost importance. I repeat, no vegetables to foreigners."

We finally were directed to a small shed where a woman was butchering what we thought was perhaps a goat. Justin (the vegetarian) waited outside as I asked for vegetables. As she expertly sawed away at what looked like part of a thigh, she stated that she, in fact, had no vegetables. I asked her about the tomatoes, carrot, and onions she had on the floor. She gave me an "oh, those" look, and gave us a uniform price per kilo for all the vegetables. As Justin waited outside looking ill, she bagged, with bloody hands of course, her vegetables into a plastic bag, also covered in blood. I paid her and she went back to her butchering job. Well that was easy enough...not!! With bloody vegetables in hand, we thankfully began our descent.

It was time to leave civilization again. We bought some more essentials (water and chocolates) and headed back to our boats, leaving this wonderfully unique tourist outpost for the smelly but free confines of our kayak. On the way down, we passed the *Fuente Del Inca* and decided to pass again on drinking from it. The possibility of dysentery, no matter how unlikely, overruled the attraction. I suppose we're not as adventurous as we were in our youth. When we arrived back to our boats, we packed up quickly and headed out for day three of our sirena search.

We paddled past our first campsite and headed to the north side of the island (away from the Isla de la Luna) towards the most barren and uninhabited part of the island. Again, as we paddled, the landscape alternated from sloping hills on one side of a peninsula to shear rock faces on the other side. The rocky outcroppings were the most interesting for paddling, as they took on contorted and diverse shapes. Some looked like human faces, one reminding me of my father, who had passed away a few years back. In a way, it felt as if the rocks we were passing were all my ancestors, reminding me of the immensity of time that has passed from their creation to the present moment of myself floating beneath them. These rock faces silently and stoically stared down at me; I stared back in reverence. I had assumed that the paddling would be along a shoreline of dusty, featureless rolling hills but I was delightfully proven wrong. Every point had little beaches or small rocky caves, and I was happy to see the potential for sirenando on every curve of the island. This side of the island was much less populated, with only a few dwellings scattered here and there along the coast. The weather was again ideal, with no wind and cool pleasant temperatures – except that the sun's bright reflection off the lake began to get uncomfortable.

The glare was so bright, I could hardly glance at the surface of the lake without feeling my retinas complain. I began wearing two sets of sunglasses wrapped together with a shoelace to stop the glare. I would often forget that I looked like the classic nerd with broken glasses, but Justin reminded me whenever possible.

With our poorly detailed map, each corner we turned was a surprise, revealing the details of a calm slope or a rocky shore. Around one corner we saw in the distance a dark-yellow, gently sloping hill, with what looked like a long beach below it. We headed straight for this intriguing strip of land. While paddling there, we saw a lone fisherman and asked if he had caught any fish. The sad reply, *"no hay."* We hadn't had a bite either, but we believed that was from our inexperience. It now seemed as if perhaps the fishing in this part of the lake was a bust altogether, and not just with the trucha. On the way to the beach we were aiming for, we came across an idyllic-looking hidden cove with a tiny beach that looked so serene and peaceful we had to check it out. It turned out to be a spot custom-made just for us with space for our kayak, two tents and not much else. The shallow beach allowed us to bring our gear up and away from the water, as we were now aware of the Titicaca

High fashion sunglasses

wind tides. There was also an outcropping of rocks with various perches to play our music for attracting prospective sirenas.

Because we arrived earlier than expected, we were able to enjoy the afternoon sun and try our hand at fishing from the shore. We would beat the odds and catch the elusive trucha. Hemmingways of Titicaca were we! After a pleasant half hour of throwing our lines into calm green water and catching large quantities of lake weed, the sun set and we headed in for another meal without fish. To compensate for this lack of protein, we began cooking some of our new "slaughterhouse" vegetables. Sounds like a name for a vegan punk rock band, The Slaughterhouse Vegetables.

4
The Song Revealed

After eating in the calm before the night's inevitable winds, Justin went off investigating the island on foot, while I looked for somewhere to play my charango to get a musical sense of the area. We both had our own way of connecting to the surroundings and it was important to have time to explore in our own unique way. Traveling with someone involves long periods of shared intensiveness, and it is vital to find little periods of time apart to create one's own mini-narrative not colored by the other. These varied experiences can also lead to wonderful stories at the end of the day.

As Justin often took these hikes at sunset, I was always entertained with tales of mysterious shadows and whistling winds in the dying light of desolate hilltops. My stories were usually the same. I played my charango at the water's edge watching the wind and sun create collages of texture and color, inspiring the musical collaboration between the lake and me.

With these nightly sessions, I began to understand music creation on a new level. Most of my musical ideas have come from specific experiences or from wandering daydreams, but here I was concentrating on what physically lay in front of me for inspiration. It was almost as if I were watching a cut of a movie and I was creating the soundtrack. I just let my hands follow my mind as I gazed at the blue to green to grey water swirling with the breezes and current, as sunlight sparkled on the surface in the fading afternoon light. It was something I realize I hadn't taken much time to do in my life, so filled with rushing around. Here we had time to just observe and watch. Taking hours of one's day to just watch the scenery is unheard of and economically probably impossible for most people. Even vacations are filled with itineraries to fill in the days. Just sitting, observing and strumming was immensely relaxing, and I was happy to see how effortlessly musical ideas form with such stillness. It was a true meditation to not force ideas and to let my thoughts coincide with what was immediately in front of me. To receive inspiration from the surroundings, I had to tune in to it on its own frequency. It felt like my body feels when doing endurance exercises such as long distance paddling or swimming. You just get in the zone and let yourself go.

One of my most memorable "zone" moments was ocean swimming with my friend Jeff. While we were students at the University of California, Santa Barbara, he and I would make a half mile swim from "Campus Point" to Goleta Pier three times a week in the late spring and summer. We were already great friends, but the swimming got us into this amazing "water bond." We swam at the same speed, and as he was left-handed, and I was right, we swam in unison and faced each other as we swam. Stroke for stroke we sped along the water. There is always the thrill of the unknown while swimming in the ocean (what exactly is underneath us!), but swimming with my friend took some of this nervousness out of my stroke, and I just concentrated on my body flying through the water. Through waves, wind, or deep blue calm, we were always swimming right next to each other, perfectly in tune with each other's pace. It always felt as if we were moving much faster than if we had swum alone, although after timing ourselves, this wasn't true; in fact, sometimes we were slower. Probably this was because while swimming alone, getting to the finish point was more important. We wanted to get out of the water that was filled with the "unknown." With Jeff, it felt as if we could swim forever. Our combined efforts seemed to refuel us, and after we had finished, we couldn't believe how effortless the swim had been. We were like the schools of fish that swim the seas in perfect unison.

Now, playing my charango to the water, I began to feel a unity with my surroundings that I had only previously felt with such adventure sports. A new door of interacting with the world was opening up. The song that I had been playing the previous night was the melody I returned to as I sat on a little sandy beach at our campsite, watching the water patterns before me. The patterns felt like musical charts that I had to follow along and read. The wave patterns were so rhythmic, I began to wonder if all bodies of water had their own particular rhythms? Would a song created on a beach in India have a different rhythmic feel than one created on a beach in Santa Cruz. Like playing with different drummers, I realized that the pulse of the planet is definitely not uniform, and the rhythmic possibilities of water is endless. As my sirena song began to form, I began to feel a significant change in my relationship to the lake. Sometimes songs performed in front of an audience take on a life of their own, becoming more transcendent with the reaction, quiet or vocal, of the audience. The exchange becomes equal and interdependent. I felt that my charango song was becoming increasingly interdependent on the lake before me.

At the end of my charango strumming session, as the sun set beside the tranquil water of Lake Titicaca, if felt like the best part of me was being offered to this place. In turn, this place was offering me peace and beauty. There was an equality in the exchange that I found exhilarating and hopeful. I hoped that perhaps the sirens of the lake could also hear the song and join in the musical dialogue, a jam session between a water spirit, the lake and a human. This was an intriguing change from the usual siren story; I was trying to entice the sirens to listen to my music. It felt like going to a very important and daunting audition. Because this was a small beach surrounded by totora reeds, there didn't seem to be a good place to leave my charango overnight, so I decided to take my charango into my tent for the night and try sirenando another time. There would be other opportunities to find a perch, and I felt my "sirena song" was not yet written.

We got up in the morning (Justin still a little sore in the wrist), packed up our boat and headed around a new point towards new discoveries. We didn't see anybody – no buildings, roads or boats as we paddled in the light breeze, only the ever-present terraced lines that surrounded the island. After a few hours, we curved around a rocky point to a beach that was absolutely breathtaking. It was a gradual beach so the colors were an amazing template of blues moving to greens. Justin thought it looked like a tropical beach where you had to wear a woolen hat. It was also the biggest beach we had seen, probably 200 yards long, and, most importantly, there were visible caves and places to camp.

Up above on the ridge, we saw a ruin called *La Chincana* (The Labyrinth), which according to our guidebook contained a series of

Tropical beach at 12,000 feet

interconnected rooms and passageways thought to be storehouses for ceremonial maize. The rooms had also housed *mamaconas* (virgins of the Sun), women specifically chosen for their purity, who made *chicha* (a sacred fermented corn drink) and wove cloth for use in rituals presided over by the spiritual leaders of the island. I was imagining drinking *chicha* with *mamacones* while overlooking this sacred lake when I was unfortunately interrupted midway through this blissful daydream with a splash by Justin's kayak paddle. We were headed in for a beach landing.

  It was probably for the best that my daydream was halted as I have had one really bad experience drinking a homemade *chicha*. This occurred while traveling with my band on my previous trip to the Andes and produced the worst hangover of my life. It started out simple enough. A local musician offered us *chicha* and so as not to offend him, we drank some. The only problem was that three of my band members did not drink alcohol, so they slipped the drinks to me when the man wasn't looking. I usually can hold my liquor well and rarely get drunk, or so I thought. The next thing I knew I was dancing by my sweaty self, stumbling and swirling to

Andean beats, while watching Gwynne dance with the musician (a little too close, I thought). The next thing I knew, I was underneath our van (how I got there, I don't know), listening to the musician try to convince Gwynne to go home with him. Luckily she didn't go with him, or I would have had to crawl out from under the van and dry heave on him – that would have shown him. I was sick for three or four days after that and was only kept alive by eating jello (so soothing, so red) and lying horizontally in the back of the van.

Justin and I brought our boats up toward shore, hypnotized by the clarity of the almost Caribbean-looking transparent water. We took off our clothes and jumped into the refreshing 50-degree water. While in the water, we noticed that there were some tourists up at the top of the cliffs where the ruins were located. The pristine view of an ancient ruin located on this sacred island was perhaps slightly diminished by the sight of a big blue kayak with its insides spread out and our unclothed blindingly white skin. This beach, truly one of the most picturesque I have seen, had now become our messy dorm room. Realizing this, we put our clothes on, quickly gathered our stuff, and tried to straighten up as much as possible. Unfortunately, to the sightseeing tourist, I imagine we were still an inescapable blight on their visual experience.

5
Unsettling Caves

As the sun began to set, the tourists headed back to town and we were left to ourselves. According to our tried and true schedule, Justin again went exploring while I looked for a sirena spot. There was a small cave on the right side of the beach which I had noticed while we were paddling in. As I walked towards it, my heart raced. It seemed to be the kind of cave (small and deep) that I had imagined so many times in my mind, but had not yet seen. As I got closer, it appeared that others had been using this cave for offerings as well, as there were burnt candle nubs spread on the sand. It was as if I had just walked into someone's private altar. I had a sense that this was the local's place for spiritual practices. As in other such culturally specific spiritual spots I had visited, I felt out of place. It was quickly apparent that this was not a place for me to have my own personal sirena experience. I've had this overwhelming feeling of spiritual displacement before.

While in a cave in Guatemala, I was led by a Mayan guide down a steep dark path into a chamber that was supposed to have some interesting ancient drawings on the walls. Some people in the nearby community had said it was an entrance into the Mayan underworld. When the guide led my friend and me into the cave, I immediately sensed that we shouldn't be there. I noticed many altars burning with *copal* incense and candles, signifying to me that this place was hallowed ground...a sacred place that I would be unable to properly appreciate. Down we went into the cave with gruff prodding from our increasingly menacing-looking guide. It got darker, and the guide kept racing ahead, leaving my friend and me frantically trying to keep up with the dim light of his flashlight. We turned a corner, and he shouted abruptly for us to look at a series of ancient cave drawings, pornographic in nature, while smiling devilishly. What was he up to? We felt an incredible urge to run, not walk, out of the cave into the light and the sanity of blue skies and sunshine. He reluctantly led us slowly out of the cave, and we felt immense relief when we felt the sunshine on our skin again.

As I walked away from the cave on Isla del Sol, I realized that the relationship of a person to a "sacred" place has to be personalized and contextualized. Why should anyone feel closer to God within a church, mosque or temple? I personally always feel the most religious or spiritual when I am in the ocean. I feel immersed in something so much greater than myself, rejoicing in my infinitesimal yet essential place in this life. On Isla del Sol, I did not want to feel like a tourist looking at a sacred spot belonging to "others." I wanted to feel my own unique connection to the landscape in which I was traveling – a connection that bypassed any feeling of foreignness. Could I feel as closely a part of this landscape as I did in my home of Santa Cruz? Could I develop a spiritual connection to a place that I was just visiting? Perhaps this happens when we find our own unique way of experiencing a specific place and some way to express this bond. It might be taking deep breaths, walking, running or surfing. I was becoming spiritually connected to Isla del Sol by playing the charango and creating music to fit the space. An expression that was purely from my own experience, just as genuine as someone who had cultural roots to this piece of earth by the lake. Or so I wished to believe.

As I left the much-used cave of offerings, I could feel myself becoming lighter with each step. That cave had a strange, unwelcoming "not-for-tourists – keep out" vibe. Having less knowledge of the island now seemed like a good philosophy for finding the *huacas*, as our connection to them needed to be based on gut reaction rather then pursuing hearsay. I imagine that if I had asked a locals about a cave for sirenando, I would have been led to this very cave. Or perhaps not. Maybe it was a place just for local Aymara and I was not welcome there, which is perhaps why I felt so uncomfortable.

I decided to head down the opposite side of the beach to find a place to play my charango. After a short walk on the white sand, the beach transitioned to rocky shore. There I discovered a cave tucked inside the steep cliff walls just the right size for my charango. It was more an indentation than a cave, but seemed promising for a sirena to come visit. It was a gorgeous sunset that evening with purple red streaks capturing the first bright stars in the twilight sky. I sat on a rock overlooking the lake watching the colors unfold as I played my song, already so familiar and a part of me. I played it over and over until it became like breath and blood.

When I stopped playing, it was quiet, like an empty church. I slowly stood up and left my offering, my charango, with the case open in the cave and headed back to camp. I had started to worry a bit about the whereabouts of Justin in the growing darkness, but he showed up with the same look on his face as I imagined I had – wild bliss. This was why we were here, to feel the spirit and the wildness of place and of ourselves. The layers were coming off. Like shedding our clothes to bathe earlier, our minds were naked and refreshed, the layers of inhibition flying off.

Justin's nightly sunset explorations

Our dinner was cheese, onions, potatoes and chocolate, what else, but still excellent! As everyone knows, camping food always tastes much better because of the rugged circumstances. A good example of this was my insistence that "Tang"-flavored cheesecake was the best dessert. I had made this concoction while camping in the canyons of Utah for a college field course, and when I came home for the summer to visit my parents, I insisted on making this for them. They were not as impressed. Was this what I was learning in college!?

We went to sleep as the wind began to blow its Wagnerian symphonic gale. I stayed up trying to write a bit in my journal and wondering about the strange cave that I had visited earlier. The strange feeling disturbed my ease, and I had a restless night in which the wind's groans created a bizarre soundtrack to unsettling dreams.

6
Sacred Rocks

The next morning we woke up to the silence of calm water, which was again a complete contrast to the previous night's crazy winds and accompanying spirits swirling around the tents. I peaked my head out of the tent and saw that our tropical-looking beach at 12,000 feet was covered in frost! Putting on my warmest clothes, I headed over to my little cave in the cliffs to see how my charango fared during the night. Again I had left it inside its open case, which unfortunately had blown closed. My charango was still in tune and sounded beautiful, but I didn't notice any change from previous days of playing it. I sat and played before the mirror-like lake for a bit and then headed back to camp for breakfast and to discuss the day's plan.

This was the morning that we decided to walk to Challapampa, another small town on Isla del Sol. We put on our "city clothes" (pants and shirt instead of shorts and rash guard) and carried backpacks to bring back the much-needed fresh water, vegetables and chocolate that had become our staple (*no hay trucha*!). I also carried my charango in case we met a charango player in town, and because I felt uncomfortable leaving it on the beach with so much tourist traffic visiting the ruins nearby.

We laboriously hiked up the hill to the ruins where Justin had been the night before. I was completely winded by the time I got up to the top of the ridge overlooking our beach. Head and heart pounding, I needed to rest. The *Chincana* ruins were a series of stone cut hallways that were quite small, maybe four feet high, so you had to duck through them. They led through a series of zigzags that ended in wonderful views of the lake. Justin spoke of his previous day's visit up here and the sense of energy that was powerful enough for him to feel a bit uneasy, as if the priests and attendant spirits were lurking in the shadows. It was still early in the morning and quite cold, which combined with "spirit" talk caused me to pull my clothes closer about me.

View from La Chincana – the Labyrinth

Up above the *Chincana* labyrinth, we walked on a rock path built over 800 years ago. White from sun and wear, it was a picturesque path with 360-degree views around the island. You could see bone-dry Peru on one side and the snow-capped *Cordillera Real* of Bolivia on the other. The air was exceptionally clean and pure, each breath felt like it was clearing away years of accumulated smog and dust. As we headed out of the ruins we met up with two older Aymara men who were setting up their spot to extract a toll from people visiting the sacred rock, *Titikala,* which marks the spot where the Inca creator *Viracocha* is believed to have released the sun.

At the height of Incan power, and still to this day, the rock was the most important and sacred spot on the island, and one of the most important Incan spiritual sites. For many, the pilgrimage made over hundreds of miles ended here. We were told that for the initiated there were ceremonies, especially during the winter and summer solstices, where as one passed across the island there would be elaborate rituals involving dance, music and colorful costumes. I was curious if such ceremonies still occurred on the island.

When I asked a local later in the trip, I got a one word answer, "si" with no elaboration. Perhaps just as in the height of the Incan empire, only the chosen few, those especialy initiated into the higher spiritual realms of Incan society, were allowed to participate. I still would have loved to witness such a celebration.

Now it was just Justin, myself and the rock outcropping made of reddish sandstone, indistinguishable from other such formations. I loved how this reddish rock was as holy as any cathedral in the world, and yet if the two old men had not been here to show us, we could have passed it without even knowing. There were no signs or plaques announcing the importance of the stone. I quite liked the informality of it all. Back in the States there would have been a sacred rock café and miniature *Titikala* rocks made of plastic for sale. Here the location was unadorned and completely accessible.

I am wary of "holy sites" that are made accessible only to elites. While in Guatemala, it felt wonderful to roam the ancient temples where only priests and royalty were previously allowed. Religious hierarchies have always seemed sacrilegious to me. Isn't everyone equal in the eyes of God/Goddess/Gods?

Footprints of the Gods

We passed some indentations in the nearby rocks that we later learned were called *Huellas Del Sol,* which translates to "Footprints of the Gods." It is believed by some that these giant footprints were made by the Sun after emerging from the sacred rock. I love this visual, tangible evidence of the emergence of a deity: of course he emerged from this area – here are his footprints for goodness sake!

Even with the humble presentation, Titicala is still a destination for tourists, and that was why the two old men were stationed nearby. They were endearingly grumpy, and after paying the entrance fee (to walk past them) you received no further information. We later learned that guides came from the nearby villages to give an orientation for the tourists. We were just there too early, it seemed.

We told the Aymara men that we would be returning in the afternoon since we were camped on the beach below them. I also asked them if they wanted anything from town and they requested egg sandwiches. I noticed a woman sitting by herself nearby and asked one of the men if she was his wife. With a nod, he said she was. I asked if she would want a sandwich as well, to which he replied with a neutral grunt as if she didn't even merit consideration for such a thing. I was tempted to bring back a sandwich only for her. He probably didn't believe that I would return anyway.

We continued hiking over the bleached and barren rock on the top of the island, searching for possible places to camp over the next couple of days. Most beaches were difficult to see because the cliffs were too steep. After a while we started to pass more people. Some were tourists (mostly Italian for some reason), but as we got closer to Challapampa we ran into more locals, mostly children and woman who were out walking their goats and llamas. We met some kids asking for money to take a photo of them, which was economically understandable, but not something we wanted to do. Instead, I replied that I had a picture of my home that I would like to give to them and handed them the postcard of Santa Cruz with waves crashing against a cliff next to a lighthouse. The kids looked at me bewildered. This was not the exchange they had anticipated, but they giggled and thanked me anyway. Although in hindsight

The road to Challapampa

I'm sure they would have preferred the money, I thought this was a much better interaction than taking an awkward photo.

Traveling, by definition, means you have the luxury of some disposable income. The modern traveler is not faced with the decision whether to eat or to travel. The cost of an airplane ticket alone is the equivalent to some people's yearly income. Not surprisingly, it is often expected, rightly or wrongly, that the traveler owes something to the people they are visiting.

"Give us some of your wealth," they ask or plead.

"Give me a dollar!"

"Can I have your camera?"

"How about your shoes?"

Once while traveling with a tour group in a rural town in Nicaragua, one of my fellow travelers decided to hand out pencils to the kids who were amassing around us. Her idea was to give something that would be useful to them, and she had heard that educational supplies were hard to come by. Her intention was to give a pencil to every child, but soon there was a growing mob of children around her. Even though she valiantly tried to explain in her broken Spanish that it was to be one pencil per child, they were not having any of it. Kids were grabbing at her hands faster than she could hand out the pencils. She then panicked. I'll always remember the vision of hundreds of pencils sailing through the air, like little arrows, arching down to the tiny brown waiting hands as she tossed them over her head. Thank god they weren't sharpened yet. The kids piled on the pencils as she made a hasty escape into a nearby hotel.

As we headed into Challapampa, a small town of probably a couple of hundred people, life was going on as usual. Goats and llamas wandered the street, radios blared and colorful clothes dried on strings hanging from windows. This quiet and sleepy atmosphere changed quickly with the distant sounds of motorboats fast approaching. As we walked up to the waterfront, three boatloads of tourists arrived, ready to have breakfast or take the couple of hours walk to the ruins where we were camped.

Guard llama of Challapampa

Most of the arriving travelers crowded themselves into a few waterfront restaurants. We decided to find a quieter, less crowded place to eat, not because we felt particularly different (kayak gods!), but because the current group of tourists were decidedly odd. For example, there was one group of four raggedy men and one woman, all with tattoos, scowls and cigarettes, sitting down at a table. One man was toting around a tiny monkey on a rope. The poor creature looked miserable. When this motley crew sat down, they didn't talk but seemed to brood and be "on display," and as we were not "shopping" for such company we decided to pass on by. We found a small courtyard with tables and asked if they served breakfast. A beautiful, smiling woman said they did serve "Desayuna Americano" which we assumed equaled tea, toast and eggs like the restaurant in Yumani, their vision of an American breakfast. I'm glad they could not visualize the true gluttony (mounds of pancakes with syrup, hash browns, three egg omelets, café latte's with a donut aperitif) that unfortunately for many is the true "American breakfast."

7
Proper Forms of *Sirenando*

As we waited for our tea, a man came out and asked questions about where we were from and how long we were going to stay in Bolivia. We told him of our search for "special" places to leave our instruments. His eyes lit up, and he proceeded to tell us that he was in fact also a charango player. I let him play mine with his thick, calloused hands, and sounds I had never heard before came from my charango. My strums are fast and light-handed, his were short, staccato hard jabs made partially because of his thick hand, but also a result of a relationship with the instrument much different than my own. It was so odd to hear the tone of my instrument change in his hands. Odd, yet wonderful. I played him

Fellow charango player

a song with my own "style," and he beamed. Same instrument played with different hands, and different styles, but with a mutual affection and respect for this beautiful instrument. I had a similar experience on the island of Hawaii, but unfortunately with different results.

While visiting some friends on this beautiful island, the birth place of the Ukulele, I was asked to sit in with a Hawaiian band, who had been told I was a musician. I did not bring an instrument, so I was kindly lent a ukulele. The musicians asked me what I wanted to play, and I said I knew some easy three or four-chord South American songs that would be easy for them to follow along with. They enthusiastically played along to the fast rhythms of my ukulele playing. Essentially, I was playing the charango on a ukulele, strumming spastically with blurring hands. The man who had lent me the ukulele was waving his arms in encouragement, or at least I thought. After playing, with thunderous applause from the audience, I proudly walked over to the man and waited to be pronounced a musical genius when I realized he looked as if he was going to punch me in the face.

"How dare you play my *uke* like that!," he said red-faced.

"You have to caress the instrument, it looked like you were trying kill it," he continued, with steam coming out of his ears. "That wasn't cool, now give it back!"

I slunk out of there feeling decidedly unmusical.

On Isla del Sol, I couldn't be happier to have this vivacious man put his island energy into my charango. After treating us to a small concert, he listened to our attempts at sirenando, looking at us increasingly like we were misbehaving children. We had been going about it all wrong, he sternly told us. One has to put the charango by itself (he was incredulous about my idea of leaving the charango inside of the case) into a cave at night, after midnight to be exact, and pick up the charango before the sun rises. I asked if we needed to give any kind of offering to the sirena, and he said we should put something of great personal value beside the charango. He also said that there were some very powerful places on the island, and when I described to him the cave with the candle offerings near the labyrinth ruins, he said that this was a much-used *huaca* for the local fishermen. He also insisted that there were many others on the island, hundreds even! The island itself was a *huaca*. He said that he, as well as his ancestors, had been to many these of *huacas* and that they were all very powerful. I asked him if my charango would sound different after being left by a *huaca*, and he said, "*Por supuesto*" (of course), if I followed his instructions.

The food was delicious, and he was a truly delightful host with a ready laugh, which, to be honest, was unique among the locals we had met thus far. It often seems like the last cultural bridge to be allowed across is the one of humor. Sometimes humor doesn't translate well, or is too culturally specific to understand completely, but I think it is also a cultural refuge, a safe place to hold on to one's cultural identity.

One of my favorite traveler stories came from a musician who worked with Andean street performers in major cities around the world. He said they would often pepper their folkloric songs, which to the passersby seemed to illustrate aspects of the indigenous rural lifestyle – with slang (hopefully unintelligible to the audience) about recent amorous activities or drunken nights out on the town. The gathered audience saw and heard only what the musicians wanted them to hear and understand, the indigenous "faraway" descriptions of Andean mountain life. All the while, they were trying to keep a straight face about the fact that they were also singing about falling down drunk at a local bar. After all, these musicians were often teenagers. As cultural outsiders, we are only privy to what is offered us.

8
Phone Home

Before we left Challapampa, we tried to make a phone call. We learned that the only cell phone for public use was at the top of the stairs in a local woman's home. A pig snorted around noisily at the bottom of the stairs as we walked up the rickety stairs to attempt to communicate with another world. It was strange to see cell phones on Isla del Sol as the island seemed so ancient and far away from modern accouterments, but we were very happy these communication technologies were available. We hadn't talked with our wives and children since Copacabana, and even there it had been rushed and awkward with weird acoustic echoes and loud homesick voices, speaking a mile-a-minute in the next booth. We really wanted to hear our family's voice, and let them know we loved and missed them.

With cell phone reception intermittent when traveling to distant lands, often all you can hope to say is, "HELLO...WE'RE ALIVE...LOVE YOU...GOODBYE!!!"

Anything beyond that is pushing it. Conversations can be somewhat strained in these situations anyway. Attempts at trying to illustrate the beauty, uniqueness or hardships of traveling are often met with empty silence. The person on the other line can not enter this world, especially when he or she is at the moment trying to clean up scrambled eggs from the floor or trying to get the dogs from barking at the postman, as we knew was the case with our patient wives. That said, I knew our families were anxious to learn of our safety.

Our phone calls passed through the airwaves and satellites to our homes and we both were able to give brief hellos to our wives and children. Dazed, with our heartstrings pulled three thousand miles away, we were ready to leave Challapampa with its cell phones, monkeys on ropes and charango-playing waiters.

Heading back up the trail to the ruins, we passed groups of tourists on their way back to their tour boats. We probably wouldn't

Leaving Challapampa

be seeing many people for the next few days, so we were getting our fill now. Arriving back to the ridge overlooking our boats, we delivered the promised egg sandwiches to the surprised but still grumpy old men, saving the biggest sandwich for the wife. As we stood gazing at the island from one of its highest points, we fell under the trance of three small islands in the horizon, a few miles north of our camping beach. On our simple map they were nameless and looked much smaller then they appeared in real life. We wondered if they were visited often, and if someone might live on them. Perhaps we could camp on one of them. We both agreed to head out to those islands in hopes of finding one with a good camping beach. We walked past the sacred rock, the labyrinth, and down to the beach to our beloved kayak, which would take us to our next adventure. We loaded up quickly as we now had the packing down to a science, and began paddling for the small islands. We took one last look at this wonderful spot, worthy of any travel brochure, but thankfully with no Club Med…yet.

9

Mysterious Islands

The first island we paddled to we named "Inca Head" island because the side profile of the island looked very much like the stereotypical carvings of Incan heads with long sloping foreheads we had seen so often in the tourist shops. The island was a quarter of a mile from our campsite, so it did not take long to arrive on its shores. It was again the high, craggy rock limestone formations that we loved to paddle by with each section displaying its own unique rock face. We passed around the backside away from Isla del Sol to see that it was, in fact, a narrow island, maybe 200 yards across with little caves and arches lining its half-mile length. It was a rugged-looking island that would not have been out of place in Baja, California. There didn't appear to be any place to camp, so when we arrived at the end of this island, we decided to press on to the next one, which from a distance looked like a hat. "We shall call it Hat Island," Justin sagely pronounced.

The paddle from Inca Head to Hat Island was about a mile long, and as we came closer, we saw a huge cave, unlike any we had seen so far. Excited, we headed right for it. As we approached the opening, we realized it must be quite big because we could not see the back end of it. We cautiously paddled into it taking pictures of curious rock formations inside, but the deeper we ventured in, the more uneasy we felt. It was dank-smelling and dark, with strange echoes coming from deep within the cave. How far back did the cave go – dare we go further? What was that sound? Our double kayak was quite long, about seventeen feet, and we became increasingly concerned about scraping a hole in our boat as the cave became restrictively smaller the further we went in. Still, we silently and cautiously felt drawn deeper inside the cave.

There are many caves on the Northern California coast where I live, and I always feel drawn to them as well. One cave near my home, a natural tunnel actually, seems to call me, siren-like, any time I pass near it. It is a foreboding-looking cave with waves crashing all around. It feels as if I am in a trance at times as I pass through the musty, salty rock entrance. It can be quite dangerous, and you have to time the entry just right. You must wait for a small-size wave to take you into the cave, and then you must wait in the middle with all the roaring of the wild ocean surrounding you, until another surge of waves carries you out the other end. On stormy days it is very dangerous to enter with a real possibility of getting smashed up onto the cave's walls. On those days when I know it is almost suicidal to consider entering, I still feel the call and have to fight the will to enter. I can feel my adrenaline surging as the reckless part of me pushes me into the watery womb of the cave. As my self-preserving better sense kicks in, I also feel a true sense of loss – a missed opportunity to feel intensely wild.

The cave on Hat Island beckoned us further, but as we inched forward, our boat began to rub and scratch along the cave walls, so we decided reluctantly to paddle backwards out into the wider entrance. It's amazing how just this few-minute side-trip into the center of the island so quickly took on mystical dimensions. Both Justin and I were wide-eyed and more than a little bit spooked as we entered a world where we would not have been surprised to see dragons, pirate gold, skeletons or sirens. With each day on Lake Titicaca, the mystical and supernatural was becoming more plausible. Our bodies were also strengthening from paddling and hiking and we were feeling more "animal-like." The physical and the spiritual possibilities of being human were less atrophied than they had been in quite a while for both of us.

We left the mystical "Hat Island" and headed for the strangest island of them all, one that was unnaturally flat as if it had been sheared off with bulldozers. It was getting late in the day, and we were still hoping to find a little island to camp on. The apparent flatness of this island made camping and sleeping comfortably a distinct possibility. Camping on one of these small islands was attractive on many levels; it would mean we might have the island to ourselves, and it afforded us a look at an area that most people visiting Isla del Sol would never see.

As we paddled to this new flat island, we were surprised to see some small man-made structures covered in aerials and antennas.

We landed at a small area between rocks where we could anchor our boat and hop out. As we stepped onto the island, we were met with a strange landscape. There was virtually no vegetation across the entire flat top of the island except for hundreds of burnt-looking, foot-high cactus. We walked over to the chain-link fence enclosure with the antennas, wires and metal gadgets and couldn't figure out what they were being used for, or if they were still in use. It was very low-tech machinery, such as might have been used for weather surveillance. We decided to survey the rest of the island, which turned out to be completely flat.

The blackened knee-high prickly plants were everywhere. And if being poked in the ankle repeatedly by these spiny plants wasn't enough, most of them were covered with prodigious amounts of spider webs that attached to our shoes and legs as we walked. It was a minefield of the sticky and prickly. And it was hot, so add sweat to the mixture. More disconcerting, as we walked we noticed that there were a lot of bones scattered about that could have been from goat, cow, or perhaps llama. However, they didn't appear to be human (good news!). We made our way to the side of the island closest to Isla del Sol and discovered a series of mounds. These mounds were about a foot high and were surrounded by more bones. Was this some kind of animal graveyard? It began to feel a little eerie. The idea that we might spend the night here now became inconceivable and just getting the hell off the island became the more attractive and necessary option. It felt like the island of Dr. Moreau with science experiments gone amuck with mysterious mounds surrounded by bones, burnt cactuses and spider webs with no spiders. We hurried (read *sprinted*) back to our boat, and without a moment's discussion, jumped in and paddled quickly back to the safety of the Isla del Sol.

After a few strokes of my paddle, I felt something crawling on my legs. With panic in my voice, I told Justin that I had to take off my spray skirt to check out who the stowaway creature was. While I was trying to get access to my legs, which were crammed into the boat surrounded by our equipment, I felt something bite me. I emitted a tiny yelp and then a much louder, "SHIT." The bite itself was not too intense but I wondered about the after effects. Was some sort of venom now heading towards my heart and brain, soon to render me paralyzed? I was panicked and with good reason as I have had experiences with South American poisonous bugs before.

I contracted a particularly nasty tropical disease called Leishmaniases while working in the Amazon, which is a parasitical infection caused by a sand flea. Lesions and destruction of cartilage were the symptoms, and there was no cure. Massive injections of sodium antimony, a heavy metal, were injected into my bloodstream to effectively kill the parasite before it ate me from inside out. I received "treatments" from an infectious disease researcher from the Amazon Research institute (INPA), who treated his patients like lab rats, injecting us in the forehead, toes and fingers, anywhere lesions occurred. This was a new form of treatment, with no real known understanding of long-term effects of high levels of sodium antimony. Perhaps as a result of this, my appendix burst a few weeks after treatment. I literally barely made it home from the Amazon alive.

We guessed that what had bitten me in the kayak must have been a spider because of all the webs we passed over, although we never did find the culprit. We kept paddling, and I didn't feel any queasiness or loss of feeling in my limbs. YES! It seemed as if we made it safely off what we now called "Death Island."

After a period of time back on the water, we marveled over the remarkable differences between these three islands that were all located within a mile of each other. It felt as if we had been placed in the epic story of Homer's "*The Odyssey*" passing between bewitching islands. Relieved to be alive, we headed back to the warm, inhabited shores of Isla del Sol where we still had a bit of time before sundown to pick a beach with sirenando possibilities.

10
The Beach

When we landed back on Isla del Sol, our feet touched the finest, whitest sand we had seen yet. After our voyage to "Death Island," this place felt wonderfully welcoming. We quickly set up camp, leaving enough time to wash off in the lake and even try a spot of fishing, which now was just an exercise in futility, but none-the-less quite relaxing....like throwing a frisbee on the beach. Throw line, grab line, reel in line with nothing on it, and repeat. There probably was also the fantasy element that we might actually catch something! "*Si hay Trucha*," we would proudly proclaim! The beach was utterly quiet, secluded and, most importantly, there were caves.

The beach

Bordering the beach on both sides were small caves surrounded by freshwater springs that created lush gardens at their entrances. These caves beckoned us like mirages. In this desolate landscape of heat and dryness, they looked like little Gardens of Eden. I asked Justin if he was going to put his guitar in one of the caves, and he said that he would try the one on the left side of the beach. This is what I secretly had hoped for as the cave on the right side of the beach really called to me.

Justin in front of a hidden cave

The cave was perfect, small enough to be hidden but big enough to barely fit my charango. The lush green plants surrounding it were a sight for sore eyes after visiting "Death Island" with its dead, dried up, prickly plants. The cave was slightly curved away from the beach, and thus would protect my charango from wind and water. It looked so inviting that I couldn't imagine not wanting to visit it if I were a sirena. It also did not appear to have been recently used in ceremonies by local, as the dirt was undisturbed.

I wanted to prepare tonight's sirena offering in accordance with what I had been told by the charango player in Challapampa. I would place my charango in the cave at midnight without its case, which meant I had to stay up quite a few hours past the time

I usually went to sleep. I would also leave some offerings in the cave, something of value – perhaps the most valuable thing I carried, a piece of chocolate. I would also place a post card of Santa Cruz to present an image of the water where I felt the sirena spirit almost everyday at home. The agenda was set, and now I had to wait until midnight to see it through. As the sun began to set, I played my new song along the shore to entice the sirenas to visit that night.

As Justin and I sat down to dinner, we talked some more about the strange islands we had visited earlier that day. Each island had such a distinctive feel as if each was a different country in itself, which I suppose is a good description of all islands. We also reminisced about our loved ones. We felt very far away from our families, and we missed them. Justin was distancing himself more and more from my sirena search, just enjoying the trip on its own merits. Kayaking around Lake Titicaca can stand on its own as a great adventure. The sirena/charango search was something I had thought about for over ten years, so my belief in it had time to mature. Sirenando was, in a sense, an accumulation of all of my exposure to and experience with water and music combined. The reality of "something" occurring seemed more and more plausible as this trip progressed. I was very thankful that Justin never showed any sign of annoyance or cynicism in my belief. In his own way, I knew that he was a "believer," too. We both had spent a lot of time in the wilderness, and we did not have strong histories of organized religions to scare away any animistic/pagan beliefs in the possibilities of communing with the wild Earth. We both seemed to be caught in the spells we had felt so much in our youth, before adult life dulled the edges.

We both went to our tents and got ready for the craziness of another wind-whipped night. By this time in the trip, we both had our own way of keeping warm. My method was to get in my sleeping bag with no clothes and zip up the mummy hood tightly to keep in the warmth. Justin had a system of layering all of his jackets and clothes on top of his sleeping bag while sleeping in long johns. Once in these positions it was very difficult, mentally and physically, to get out of these cocoons of warmth, but this is just what I had to do on this night.

I stayed up reading my book, which was engrossing enough to keep me occupied (interesting enough a fictional book about Darwin's trip to the Galapagos islands, a decidedly non-mystical look at island mysteries), while keeping a vigilant look at my watch to see when I had to go outside and head to the cave. It seemed like an extremely long time waiting for midnight, but when the time came, I extracted myself from the tent's comfort, and headed into the cold darkness. The wind was really whipping now, making strange noises in the surf that sounded oddly like birds chirping. I started up the beach with my charango and headlamp turned on. After a few steps, I wondered if perhaps I should keep my headlamp off, so as not to scare away any sirenas. Perhaps she was on the beach observing somewhere. I stepped on a strip of damp lake weed and jumped, thinking for a moment it was a mermaid tail. With each step on this beautiful beach, all of my senses switched to high alert.

I finally made it to the cave I had chosen and placed my charango in the cave on top of a shirt to protect it. Next to it I lay my postcard and chocolate. It really looked like an adequate offering. The charango sat so perfectly in the cave, as if the cave had been carved over time to house it. I realized how haphazardly I had set my charango out before, without an enticing offering, and with a lackluster presentation. I proudly took one last look at my charango altar and headed back to the tent to get some sleep before I would return at 5:00 in the morning.

Back in the ten, with my clothes off in the warmth of the mummy bag, I tried to sleep. This was difficult as the howling wind and sirena possibilities created "Dali-esque" dreams of womanly walking guitars and icicle moons in my restless, half awake mind. I woke up every half hour to check my watch, and finally at about 4:45 a.m., I was ready to get my clothes on and check my instrument. It was still dark outside, so I grabbed my headlamp but kept it turned off, and headed for the cave. There it was, my charango, shining in the starry night. Beautiful. I picked it up, strummed it and it sounded different, noticeably different, and my heart raced. It sounded beautiful as always, but the sound waves vibrating through my body seemed much deeper than usual. I played some more, and with each strum this feeling only intensified. Now I was confronted with the possibility that my charango had actually been strummed by a sirena. Feeling lightheaded with adrenaline, I headed back to the tent where I could get warm and assimilate what had happened.

When I got to my tent, I fretted over whether I should have left my charango in the cave longer, if perhaps the sirena was still out there. Perhaps she hadn't finished her song, and I had scared her away! I stumbled down the beach again, wind whipping my face, to put the charango back in the cave. Halfway there I realized there was no point to this, my charango had already changed! "Get yourself together Stephen," I told myself. I was acting irrationally, most likely because of the irrationality of holding an **actual sirena's song in my hands**! Now it was time to explore the beautiful, seductive tones while they were still there. Who knows if the sound would wear off and when? At sunrise would the magic disappear? Not wanting to waste any more time, I returned to the tent.

I took off my clothes, jumped into my sleeping bag and held the charango close to my body. It lay right over my heart. When I first played it by the cave, it seemed to resonate right into my heart and I wanted to feel this again. I strummed it and my heart felt strummed as well. The vibrations and tones went deep, unusually so for such a high-pitched instrument. It rang though my body as a cello would. It was beautiful. It felt as if all channels of my body were opened. I played all five sets of doubled strings slowly, over and over again.

As I played, I realized my mind was filling up with thoughts of my family. I could hear their wonderful voices and feel their presence with each strum of my charango. Notes played resonated through my chest and beating heart, creating this incredible melody of love for my wife and son. With each strum my heart seemed to pump louder. At one point I said, "SONIA," out loud as I strummed. This was the name my wife and I had chosen for our soon-to-be-born daughter. I felt a jolt of adrenaline run though my body as I said her name. Sonia. I said it again, letting each charango string ring. My mind and heart raced as something wonderful occurred to me. The five letters of Sonia coincided with the five distinctive musical notes of the charango's paired strings, GCEAE. As the charango sang, I realized it was singing Sonia's name, S–O–N–I–A, like a morse code straight to my heart. The sirena's song was Sonia. I was going to have a girl named Sonia. The siren's song I was hearing was not a seductive call to dangerous rocks as the sirens of myth but a call to let love ring through my whole body. To listen to the heart, where songs originate, and sing its pure song...Sonia. Five letters of love from five sets of strings, strummed by my five fingers in a duet with the five fingers of a sirena.

The increasing physical sensation of love pounding out from my heart was almost overpowering. It was as if I were being taught a lesson about the human potential for love by my own heart. "You think you've felt love before, huh? Well, how about THIS!!!" The strings of the charango, like ripples on the water, intensified and spread this feeling to my whole body. It felt as if my potential for love was growing with each strum. If I wasn't so elated, I honestly might have worried I was having heart attack. I was amazed to realize that love could feel so powerful, and it felt as if I had just been taught the most important truth. The potential for love grows exponentially. The siren song had broken down the barriers of my love's limits. I became extremely aware that love only grows, grows, GROWS!!!

Words to this powerful love song began to flow out of me. I strummed the charango over my heart, playing the chords written on the shores outside my tent, and sang. The spirit was alive in me, and like those who rise up singing and who have done so throughout time, I too felt the higher calling to sing of my love for all creation. At the same time I didn't want to alarm Justin who was still asleep, so my singing was not belted out to a congregation of believers but whispered into the folds of my tent which flapped to the wind's rhythms.

By the time the suns rays warmed my tent, I had the song completed, and it was called Sonia's Song. As my body relaxed from the intensity that had burned through me in the creation of my song, I realized that the wind had completely relaxed as well. As I peeked outside the tent, I saw the sun appearing on the glassy, blue surface of the lake. Half way across the world I realized that what I was looking for, a siren's song, was growing in my wife's belly.

SONIA'S SONG
A siren song for you from a lake
A lake far, far away
A message from the heart
I'm to give to you
Love follows you always
I heard this song, knew it was for you
Tears of joy Sonia
Message came from water for my daughter
Music of sand and stone
And every day's a gift
That's what you are, something special in this world
I heard this song, knew it was for you, tears of joy, Sonia.

Not much later Justin awoke, poked his head out of his tent and asked how the sirenando went. I told him, "I think *it* happened for me" – the charango was different. I told him I had written a song for my soon-to-be-born daughter after visiting the cave in the early hours of the morning. Justin has a young daughter so he smiled, intuitively understanding the power of such a song. I felt like I couldn't say any more about the night, and he didn't ask. The silence that surrounded us for the next few hours was filled with thoughts about our families and our love for them.

11
Soaking It In

For the rest of the day, Justin and I enjoyed ourselves on the beach with no agenda. I felt emotionally spent from my wild, musical night and just wanted to bask and relax in this amazing spot, smiling at the fortune the universe had presented us. The cliffs surrounding the beach were so steep, practically vertical, we doubted anyone could even see this beach from the top of the island.

A day at the beach

I realized as I relaxed on the beach that a part of the trip had finished. The sirena had sung an amazing song for me. That song was a part of me now, etched into my heart and within the wood grains of the charango. As a songwriter, I always know when a song is finished. It always feels like a gift when it fits together musically and lyrically, with a catchy musical hook to capture the listener's attention. The good songs feel like musical miracles, and my sirena song felt exactly like one, too, a gift from the windy shores of Lake Titicaca.

People often describe their success in artistic endeavors as divine intervention, and often times I wonder where my artistic inspirations come from as they seem to arrive out of thin air. Sonia's sirena song was very different. It was a collaboration of many days with the elements of Isla Del Sol; the wind, the water and rocks, and finally the sirena. I went looking for inspiration, and she found me. Following this thought, I began to wonder how many other siren songs were there to discover in the world. If I immersed myself in other watersheds, listening to the sounds, watching the water patterns, feeling the breezes, waiting for sirens, would a new song present itself as powerful as the one from Isla del Sol?

What an exciting branch of music theory this could be, one that would be based on "environmental notation." Patterns, shapes, colors, smell, and sounds of our surroundings become the musical notes and rhythms in musical creation. Looking at a landscape would be like looking at a musical score. The more attention paid to the intricacies of our surroundings, the more virtuosic the musical creation.

What made my Isla del Sol musical experience so wonderful and revelatory was that the finished song wasn't about me and my "deep" thoughts and emotions, but was about the wonder of life outside of me; the birth of a beautiful being, Sonia. It was a song to celebrate love, which by definition is not a solitary creation.

As I sat on the beach allowing the previous night to sink into my being, I thought that I did not want this "opening up" to stop. I wanted desperately to have the magic stay inside me, and for the music to breathe through my whole being, through every pore of my body. This thought reminded me of a mythical creature of South America called Uakti.

12
Uakti

I heard about the Uakti from a musical group of the same name from Brazil. They performed their unique and exquisite music with mostly homemade wooden marimbas, flutes and odd stringed instruments. They explained before their concert that the Uakti is a mythical creature living in the Amazon with a body full of holes, and when wind passes through these holes, it creates beautiful music that entrances the listener. As the creature runs through the forest, listeners venture out to find the source of the sound, hypnotized by the entrancing notes, they disappear into the woods, some never to be seen again. I love imagining this creature running through the dark, green forest creating strange and entrancing harmonics. I also find it an interesting metaphor for this trip.

As I traveled along the coast of lake Titicaca, my body and mind continued to open up. I became more and more in touch with my surroundings and my place in these surroundings. As the trip progressed, I felt more and more "holes," like entryways, opening up in my being, allowing me to hear music within myself that had been blocked up. With the help of the sirena, I was able to interpret this opening in myself with the creation of a song. People in spiritual communities and practitioners of Indian traditional medicine often refer to such energy releases as the opening of *chakras*. *Chakras* are energy or "force" centers in specific areas on the body. When these chakras are opened, we are able to release light energy. A wonderful visual manifestation of this idea is the *uakt*i with all of its chakras open (literally), beautiful music flowing from its body! Lying on the beach on Isla del Sol, I realized that as I ran across the beach the previous night with my charango in hand, I could have been mistaken for a *uakt*i and this made me smile!

That night we ate another "wonderful" meal of half-cooked vegetables and eggs and went to sleep realizing that we might finish the circumnavigation of Isla del Sol the next day. Next on the agenda would be the crossing to Isla de la Luna, where we hoped to spend at least three days. We wanted to be there during one of the biggest festivals of the year called *Coronación de La Virgen de Copacabana*, which was occurring all around the lake. We imagined that Isla de la Luna would be the most mellow and quiet place to be. Having been to many festivals in Latin America, mellow and quiet are not adjectives I would usually use to describe them.

The next day we paddled around the rest of the island and circled some smaller islands with the hope of prolonging our time on Isla del Sol. We had passed around the island faster than we had expected, and we loved it here. We couldn't find a good place for camping on the small islands we visited, so we kept paddling. As the sun began to set, we knew we had to find someplace quickly (oh, the horror, the horror of cold hands!) and we finally landed very close to our first campsite near the town of Yumani. It was a small beach directly facing the Isla de la Luna. As we set up camp, we watched local fisherman throw out their nets to catch nothing. It must be so discouraging. I thought of all the fishermen around the world who go into waters that have been over-fished. Coming back empty-handed so often. When do they decide to give it all up? Or, do they still go out because of the spell of water, the sirens calling to them, their song in the fishermen's blood?

The next day, our plan was to get some essential supplies in Yumani, i.e., chocolate and water, and then to paddle to this island that seemed more remote than the Isla del Sol. When we first saw Isla de la Luna a week before, we were quite intimidated by it. While eating at a restaurant overlooking the lake in Yumani, it seemed like it could be a long paddle across, and potentially dangerous. If for some reason we were to run into problems and our kayak flipped, it would be a very long and cold swim to shore. The folding kayak we were using did not have airtight hatches that would allow us to turn the boat over without water completely filling it. Once our boat flipped over, it would float, but it would be completely filled with water, and thus would be very hard to bail out.

As the sun set on our last day on Isla del Sol, we watched a couple who had been washing loads of sheets (why so many sheets, we wondered?) leave the beach we were camping on and climb

Sunset on Isla del Sol

up a sheer cliff to their home at the top of the island. They had washed by hand what looked like fifty sheets and blankets and then climbed up a mile high cliff with thirty pounds of laundry, all at 12,500 feet. These people were world-class athletes, the Lance Armstrongs and Venus Williamses of Isla del Sol!

13
Yumani, Take Two

When we paddled into Yumani the next morning, there were already three or four tourist boats filled with about fifty people per boat. We received curious looks as we arrived in our boat made of cloth and unloaded our multiple bags of gear on the shore. We were invading their tourist experience with our strange, blue boat. If we had paddled in on a totora boat, we might have at least received a smile or a hand-wave but instead they just stared. A group of boys came to look at the boat and questioned us about what was inside it, and, most importantly, if they could take it out for a spin. We were uncomfortable with this for many reasons. They could flip in the cold water, and we didn't know if they could swim. Or, they could drag our kayak up against some sharp rocks, which would tear the fabric of the boat. We were also frankly in a bit of a hurry to cross to Isla de la Luna leaving enough time to find a camping spot and get a hike in before it got too cold and windy. So we had to refuse, although I did say if they would look after our boat, I would paddle

Climbing the Escalera del Inca

some of the kids around the harbor area when we got back from buying supplies. They agreed to be guardians of our tiny boat, and off we went to climb the steep, ancient Incan steps to Yumani, the *Escalera del Inca,* which is supposed to purify the climber with each oxygen-depleting step. We did not know if food and water would be easily available on Isla de la Luna, and we wanted to be prepared for that possibility.

The people of Yumani treated us much the same as they had on our previous visit, sending us on wild goose chases to find veggies (finally, found a few), promising the elusive cell phone connection home and serving us a good breakfast with service that was low on enthusiasm. We were just another group invading their town, speaking in their second language (they spoke Aymara to themselves) and asking them annoying questions like, "Can I have another tea?" or "Do you have any vegetables?"

I did meet up with one interesting character on this visit. While eating some surprisingly difficult-to-find rice at a little restaurant on the top of the island, I met this young man named Javier who was a guide for tourists. He told me he had become a tourist guide after missing the final tests to be an archaeologist, his true calling. He missed these final exams because the bus he was taking to the university was prevented from entering the capitol city La Paz due to a road blockade created by protesting farmers. The story was tragic, except for the fact he said he was making fifty times more money taking people to archaeological sights in Bolivia and Peru than he would have made as an archaeologist. He said work as an archaeologist would have meant long hours with little pay often working with foreign archaeologists who would hire him as a laborer in excavations while they wrote their academic papers.

Javier had a lot of knowledge of the area and, most importantly, was able to tell us about the three islands we had visited earlier that week. The island with the cave (Hat Island) had many stories and legends involving fishermen disappearing into the cave never to be seen again. One story that captured my imagination was about a giant horse seen inside the cave (swimming?) by a group of Japanese tourists. The horse supposedly flew out of the cave, chasing their tour boat out into the lake and flipping it over in the process. They all made it back into the boat and returned to shore to tell their story. Hey, who am I to question? I'm the one searching for a siren song.

The third island, "Death Island" as we had named it, had a more plausible story. This flat top island we learned was called Isla Quenat, and was a place where people went on occasion to give offerings to *Pachamama*, the Goddess Earth-deity of the Andean people. He said few people went to this island because it was a sacred place. I decided not to tell him of our jog across the island trampling spider webs and plants.

He was interested in our trip, but when I told him of our sirena search, he said people had all kinds of beliefs here and with a shake of his head seemed to dismiss this particular one. Perhaps he said that to me because I was a foreigner, and he felt cautious about admitting to believe in anything too "folkloric." I didn't tell him of my sirenando experience because there seemed to be no point.

14
The Gringo Road

The other interesting encounter on our second trip to Yumani was with a group of South American travelers who would have fit in quite well in Santa Cruz. The "gringo road" in South America, which I had traveled on before as a wide-eyed youth, is filled with places selling granola, Che Guevara shirts, hash pipes and the ever-present homemade jewelry. These are usually colorful wrist bracelets or interesting necklaces with big rock pendants. It always seemed strange to see young bohemians with enough money to travel setting up places on the street to sell jewelry next to the locals living in poverty trying to do the same.

Justin and I walked by this group of travelers selling their jewelry, and while Justin went in search of a cell phone (I was no match for the voice of his wife), I had a conversation with them. To be honest, I was incredibly attracted to these same people twenty years earlier when I traveled as my younger "bohemian" self. I aspired to be like these travelers with their carefree lifestyle, and I would always fall for the vagabond jewelry-making women. The femme fatales of the young traveler scene! Now much older, cautious and perhaps wiser, I usually avoided the young bohemians but was intrigued by this group because one of them had a child of about four or five years old. As I introduced myself, the boy playfully hid behind his dad's pants, and soon we were making funny faces at each other. He was wonderful, a bright light on the road, and he got me to talking about my own wonderful bright light, my son Liam. The father wondered why my family wasn't there with me. Good Question! I was struck with an intense longing to see my wife and son. I think he saw that and made no attempt to sell me anything, so we just chatted about traveling and I got some valuable information about traveling to Isla de la Luna.

Traveling without one's family is a curious practice for many cultures I have visited. In Malaysia, I always found myself at a loss for words describing why my family wasn't with me as I watched them do everything including, fish, farm, and ride motorcycles with their whole family in tow. If I told a fisherman in Malaysia I couldn't afford the plane tickets for the whole family, then he would have wondered how I had the money to take weeks off to kayak and lie around on their beaches on my own. The truth would have been even worse: I needed some time to have an adventure and "tune" into my "wild" self. He might have smiled at me then muttered in sadness about the poor, undeveloped spiritual fate of westerners.

Justin was unsuccessful in his cell phone exploration, but he did get a good workout! His already skinny frame looked even more taxed, and his sunburned face looked redder. Justin had also begun to literally lose his lips. Copious amounts of chapstick was not preventing serious splitting of his lips, which began to resemble splintered wood. I began to dread sharing a bottle of water with him as I was terrified a piece of his lip would be stuck to the nozzle.

With our bottles of water and chocolates in our backpacks, we were ready to leave Isla del Sol. As we headed down the steep ancient rock steps to the beach below, we saw a group of four Aymara men carrying a ridiculously huge piece of machinery that looked something like a tugboat motor. They had straps around it and

Getting supplies

were really struggling with the weight as they attempted to walk down the five hundred year old, cracked and uneven rock steps. As we passed them, I commented that their load looked very heavy. Not really wanting them to respond, I asked if they needed help, and they said yes....Shit!! Not that I did not want to help them, but there was a big possibility that I would hurt my back irrevocably in volunteering for this ridiculous feat. They were all just over five feet tall, close-to-the-ground people, so I immediately knew that I was going to be at a height disadvantage that would make carrying the giant piece of machinery awkward. I could anticipate my back giving out and having to lie in agony on these ancient steps for the remainder of our stay in Bolivia. Justin laughed because with his hurt wrist, he had no intention of volunteering his help. I knew I had to prove that I wasn't a weak foreigner, by God, so I toughed it out, but it was excruciatingly hard.

For the first 100 steps I was macho. Every few steps my mind was screaming for me to tell them to stop and take a break, but I said nothing. Finally with my arms straining and my back spasming I couldn't handle it any longer and yelled *"BASTA"* (enough!) Were they trying to act stoic, or did they really not feel the pain that I was feeling? They looked at me quizzically as if to say, "Is that all you got, white boy?" They spoke to each other in Aymara in hushed tones. I honestly didn't know what to do. Continue = great pain, stop = look like a wimp. We continued.

I think that they were actually embarrassed to have me there, to ask for a tourist, non-islander's help, but also truly grateful as this piece of machinery was as heavy as hell. I really was helping these people, which made me feel good and useful rather than feeling like just another foreign face looking for breakfast. While I grunted and sweated, we went farther down the high, uneven steps. I was walking like Quasimodo, trying to hold my strap level with people almost a foot shorter than me. As I had already stopped once, it was now easier to say stop again, so I did, about five more times. They smiled as my will visibly gave out and took pity on me as they offered me water while refusing to drink any themselves. They were made of heartier stuff!

While we were walking, a young local woman was walking up the hill with a bag of alpaca sweaters on her back. She stopped when she saw me (with my struggling, sweating, straining body) and asked if I wanted to buy a sweater. I realized to her I was just a walking dollar bill with arms. I understood she needed the money, and as a foreigner she thought correctly that I had money available, but really, was this the appropriate time to ask me! We finally made it to the bottom, and they humbly thanked me as I made my way back to my boat to privately, inwardly scream at my new found pains. Justin met me at the boats and privately, inwardly laughed his head off.

We loaded up our boat and were almost ready to go when one of the boys guarding our stuff reminded us about our promise to take him out in our kayak. His first request we could not honor because he wanted us to paddle him across the two miles of water to his home on the Isla de la Luna. We told him there was no room as there was no space for an extra bottle of water much less a human being, albeit a small boy. He seemed disappointed, but I did

A view of Isla de la Luna with Cordillera Real in background

take him for a quick spin around the harbor before we headed off, which seemed to satisfy our young helper. We told him we were sorry we could not carry him further but would look for him on the island when he arrived on the ferryboat. He said that we could get food there, which was encouraging, since our attempts at fishing were a bust, and the novelty of eggs with poorly-cooked potatoes was wearing off.

As was the afternoon trend, it was calm, sunny and gorgeous as we began our paddle to Isla de la Luna, which made us much less nervous about the long crossing. There still was a chance of some crazy occurrence like our boat frame breaking and us sinking, or some wild force of nature (like the famed "cave island" wild water horse attacking) but we felt quite confident we would arrive without mishap. The only obstacle to our paddle was that Justin's arm was quite sore now, so we paddled slowly. It felt good to head to an island with less boat traffic, and it seemed like the perfect getaway from the upcoming *Coronación de La Virgen de Copacabana*.

Isla de la Luna

1
Isla de la Luna

Isla de la Luna (Moon island), also sometimes called Koati, is a couple of miles west of Isla del Sol and has about 200 people living in its one small town on the eastern side of a ridge that transects the island. Looking from Isla del Sol, the island appears like a surfacing whale, long and curved. Isla de la Luna is not set up for tourism, except for ferry stops to Iñak Uyu, a well preserved temple that used to house Incan Women spiritual leaders, called *Virgenes del Sol* (Virgins of the Sun).

We arrived at the island after about two hours of straight paddling, which was quicker than we had hoped. We landed on a narrow, white stone-covered beach about a quarter of a mile from the town. We soon realized we would be sharing it with llamas and goats which were on the beach in abundance. These creatures didn't seem concerned with our presence as they continued to graze as if we were not there. There was no sign of their owners anywhere. This island was quite small compared to Isla del Sol and did not appear to have the rocky coves, arches and caves that had made such an impression on Justin and me. Isla de la Luna felt like one giant rock, surrounded by a sliver of beach.

We decided to set up camp and have a quick look around before dinner. Our goal was to spend the night at this camp and walk around the island the following day to find another camp to paddle to. Today we just wanted to walk to the town and perhaps find some fellow musicians. We felt that since this island did not get much overnight tourism, the locals might be more open to some sort of musical exchange with visiting tourists.

Putting on our dry clothes, we headed up the beach. As we walked, we could see Isla del Sol across the water, and we reminisced about our good fortune there. It was an otherworldly island, beyond our expectations, and a fulfiller of dreams. We felt very blessed to have visited it in such an intimate way. Justin talked of his sunset forays into secluded gulleys and 360-degree views of the snow-capped

Cordilleras, the dry hills of neighboring Peru, with the immense blue lake always below him. I thought of my magical charango, which I had packed into my daypack as we walked. I could almost feel the magical vibrations of the sirena song.

As we walked into the outskirts of town, we saw two young local girls wrestling and giggling as they tried to push each other into the water. They barely seemed to notice us and were having such a wonderful time, we couldn't help laughing as well. They were dressed in clothes from head to foot, which seemed conservative on this hot day, yet they were so freely pushing each other onto the beach, covering themselves in mud, laughing hysterically, that they were anything but inhibited. It was a breath of fresh air to see this open expression of pure joy. I also felt a touch of melancholy as I was reminded of wrestling with my son on Saturday mornings, with our dogs joining the fray. We realized we hadn't heard people other than ourselves laugh so openly since our paddling began. Bolivian culture outside of the city seemed humble and reserved around "outsiders." I'm sure their sense of humor was intact and richly alive outside of the theater of tourism, but unfortunately other than the charango-playing man in Challapampa, we had not witnessed much laughter. It was wonderful to hear unabashed giggling again! We walked around this happy little town that seemed to consist of a soccer field, a church and about twenty homes made of brown bricks. The soccer field looked inviting, and we thought perhaps it would be fun to play some soccer with the local players, but then a bad soccer memory brought out a twinge in my ankle.

While traveling around Costa Rica during my Peace Corps days in the late 1980s, I was asked to play with a team one afternoon in a game against a neighboring village. I'm sure they thought it would be funny to see me flail around, giving the game some added entertainment, but actually I had played soccer all of my life. I was playing reasonably well that day until my leg slipped into a hole in the ground and I heard a sickening snap in my ankle. An excruciating ride on the back of a motorcycle down a potholed road to a bus stop with another four-hour ride to the hospital left me with a cast on a broken ankle for a month. It could have been worse. Before I left the small town, I was met at the soccer field by the local *curandero* (healer) who said my foot was "out of its socket," and that he could put it back in its "right place." I argued that I was pretty sure I had broken it, what with the snap sound and the excruciating pain. The people of the community were obviously on the side of the "doctor" and thought that I was acting irresponsibly in my denial of his services. I really felt cultural walls being built brick by brick as I respectfully denied the man the opportunity to further break my ankle, possibly deforming me for life. Looking at the circle of people around me, I actually saw a person with a badly deformed arm. Was this a prior patient of the man now in front of me, I wondered? They finally let me go, and, when I eventually got to hospital to be x-rayed, my intuitions were well-founded. With this experience still in my memory and realizing it would be a long paddle to a doctor, we decided to give up our soccer match idea.

2
Pachamama Festival

Nobody paid us much attention as we wandered around the town. There was absolutely nothing for sale, and nobody seemed to want anything from us, so we just politely waved at people when we saw them. As we wandered over to a seemingly underused small, white church with shuttered windows, we saw a commotion down by the beach as two boats showed up filled with laughing people, drums and sleeping bags. We wandered over to see if we could figure out what the drums were going to be used for. Perhaps there was going to be music tonight, which would be great and exactly what we had come to town to find.

We shyly inched towards the group of ten or so people, staying to the outside so that we didn't appear to be intruding. This island felt almost as if we had walked into somebody's home. We finally got the courage to ask them if something was happening on the island that day, and if there was going to be music? They said they were going to have a *"Pachamama"* (Goddess Earth) ceremony with a shaman and people from around Bolivia, Chile, and as far away as Colombia. It was going to begin on a beach close to town and later everyone would walk to the ruins of Iñak Uyu on the other side of the island. We asked if we could come and they said *"por supuesto"* (of course) and told us to bring the instruments they saw us carrying. We couldn't believe our luck. Here we were, on an island called "Island of the Moon" where we were shortly going to celebrate the full moon and Pachamama with a South American shaman and local Aymara in a sacred ceremony. A once-in-a-lifetime opportunity!

I walked back to our camp, jumpy with anticipation. Justin, noticing this, cautioned me not to get too excited as we really didn't know what would unfold. I understood his reticence; I had noticed that some of the people getting off of the boat looked quite young, and none seemed to be locals (some with blond hair and quite tall), and yet I still was hoping the ceremony would have an element of authenticity from the Aymaran culture. I was hoping to gain more insight into the ancient connection of this place to its people.

We ate our dinner and decided to hike up to the top of the island for the sunset before we set off to the ceremony. Again, surprise, surprise, the view was gorgeous. The views of the *Cordillera Real* mountain range were stunning with sun on snow glowing in shades of purple and red. It led us to wonder how little had changed in this place. There were no roads, no electricity and no businesses. We felt privileged to be here. We took some pictures of our scruffy-bearded selves next to all of this beauty and hoped even a little of the magic would shine through in the photograph.

A smile for the family on Isla de la Luna

3
The Ceremony

We decided to wear all our available clothing for the evening ceremony because we would be walking around outside in the freezing cold for most of the night. We were curious about who would be leading the ceremony. They had mentioned a shaman coming from another part of South America, but I hoped a spiritual leader from Isla de la Luna also would be contributing to the night's proceedings. As we walked along the edge of the island, I realized how interested I was in the prospect of participating in organized spirituality, something I had not done in many years. A walk on the beach with my family was as organized as I could manage in recent times, though just as profound and spiritual as anything I've ever experienced. I still sometimes wonder, though, if perhaps I should broaden my spiritual horizon and open myself up to something outside my comfortable self-created spiritual zone. Perhaps this would be an opportunity to do so.

After a short walk, we began to hear people drumming and then, quite suddenly, we were confronted by a red-haired woman who introduced herself as a leader of the ceremony. Was she the shaman we had been told to expect? She curtly asked us where we were from, and if we had tried hallucinogenic drugs before! That's an interesting greeting, I thought to myself. She was accompanied by a professorial-looking man in his fifties, and they both anxiously awaited our response. It immediately became apparent that unfortunately, this did not seem like it was going to be an Aymaran experience after all. In fact, I sadly couldn't see any of the island people in attendance. As I peered around her, instead of the handsomely weathered, stoic faces of the local Aymara, I saw bedraggled young travelers stoned out of their minds curled into fetal positions scattered around the beach. I could almost see giant "X's" over each of their eyes. Many had taken the extremely potent vine drug from the Amazon rain forest called *ayahuasca.* The lady was speaking to us rapidly about her spiritual quests throughout South America.

The Ceremony 155

While this was commendable and quite similar to what we were doing, her lecture to us about *ayahuasca* and its importance and seeing it administered so freely here left us colder than we already were. *Ayahuasca* is not a recreational drug, as I had learned from a past experience.

I had a horrible experience with the hallucinogen *ayahuasca*, which I call "Dante's Inferno Juice" while working in the Amazon in my early twenties. The tea was offered to me by some locals without my knowledge of its hallucinogenic properties as a sort of "rite of passage." They said if I really wanted to understand the Amazon, I should drink the tea. In those innocent days of my youth I was game for anything, but I never suspected the tea would contain such a powerful drug, taking me on a never-ending nightmare journey.

After taking the tea, we went bathing in a stream as we had been in the rainforest working all day. I looked down to see my body, looking very white and hairy and suddenly ridiculously out of place surrounded by so much of the rainforest's green and brown. The short, stocky and brown Amazonians stared at me and started to laugh. I felt like a penguin in a shopping mall. Perhaps this was their purpose in having me take the drug, to help me to understand that I didn't belong here. At that point, I would have liked nothing more than to be home with my family and friends, but unfortunately there was no escaping as the hallucinogen's power deepened. The forest became a kaleidoscope of green tones, and with the darkness of night fast approaching, these colors became shadow-like and sinister, hiding malevolent spirits. I became surrounded by what felt like swirling whirlpools of dizziness and tidal waves of nausea. I got back to camp to the sounds of gales of laughter from my "workmates" and rolled myself in my hammock like a human burrito. I thought I would never return to normal, but after what felt like a century of time, I woke up in the morning more or less intact. Except for the welts (where did these come from!) and what looked like vomit underneath my hammock (hopefully mine), I felt surprisingly normal.

So here on Isla de la Luna, talk of the recreational use of this same drug sent me scurrying away from the *duena* and the professor. They looked at me with pity in their eyes and walked away disappointed. Justin felt similarly the need to distance ourselves from the zone of hallucinations, so we headed for the simpler pleasures of a campfire that was radiating much-needed warmth nearby.

The campfire was attended by people in their twenties who were singing Bob Marley and Manu Chao songs while banging on drums and passing around cups of hot tea (hopefully, not hallucinogenic). It actually was quite sweet and heartfelt, and we were warmly welcomed. Justin and I were curious about the promised ceremony, but as the night progressed and people got more and more lost in their hallucinations, we finally were too cold and frankly bored to hang out any longer. We decided to head back to our humble little camp down the beach. There was something wonderful and pure about our trip so far, finding the magic and wildness on our own, that we felt very protective of our experience. The idea of having someone else's drug-induced introduction into the spirit of this place didn't feel right. As we walked back to our campsite under the full moon, we felt completely surrounded by the spirits of this place. I hoped all of the people at the *Pacahamama* ceremony found what they were looking for as well.

4
Walking Around Isla de la Luna

The next day we slept in a bit and were awakened by the sounds of llamas nibbling the tough vegetation nearby. I opened the tent flaps and saw another sunny, beautiful day. This was the second day of the *Coronación de La Virgen de Copacabana* festivities, so it was nice to be in this pristine quiet place where we could spend the morning lying in the sun, reading and playing music. We decided to postpone our walk around the island until after lunch.

Isla de la Luna beach

At midday we packed our day bags with food and water and headed out, going in the opposite direction from the ceremony of the night before. We didn't want to run into anyone from the celebration because we didn't want to explain why we had left so early as we had sort of sneaked away without saying goodbye to anyone. As we walked, we did meet up with the boy we had met previously on the Isla del Sol. He was a serious-looking boy of about ten who went to school on the Isla del Sol and now had returned home for the holidays. He was fishing with a piece of fishing line attached to a stick, using a tiny sardine-like fish as bait. As we had seen very few people catch anything in this lake, we wondered if he had had any luck at all. He said that actually he was trying to catch a bird, pointing to the ones that were lurking about next to his baited hook. We asked him if he was planning to eat this bird, and perhaps because he saw some concern on our faces, he said that actually he planned to mount the bird on the wall. We stared at him in puzzlement. Were we translating this poorly? No, he again repeated that he wanted to mount the bird on a wall. He began to look very puzzled and perhaps guilty. When we questioned him again, he warily and slowly said that it…was…to………eat? with a questioning look in his eyes as if to ask us if this response was better. We said, *"está bien"* (yes) and then he went about "birding" again.

As we walked along the beach, it occurred to us that our bizarre interaction might have been related to how he perceived foreigners' relationship to their world. Perhaps he thought that we would look unkindly at killing a bird for food, and it would be much better in our minds to believe he was going to kill it, stuff it and mount it up on a wall for viewing – like a stag's antlers he may have seen in American movies. When he saw that this use of a bird confused us, he finally told the truth of his intentions, which was of course much more understandable than the wall mount. It was probably going to be food for his family. The idea that we would prefer to look at a dead bird on a wall rather than see him provide food for his family was sad, but we could see where it might have come from. Because he went to school on the touristy Isla Del Sol, he probably had come into contact with foreigners who were vegetarians. Thinking we might be vegetarians as well, perhaps he didn't want to offend us.

We kept walking around this serene island until we came to some ruins on the other side. There were some local people waiting for tourist boats to arrive, who were surprised to see us walking by. How did we get there, they must have wondered. They wanted to sell us some of their clay jewelry, which was quite beautiful, but it was much the same as we had seen everywhere else in Bolivia, with bright colors and pictures of condors, suns, moons and Incas designs. We bought several items from them not only because they would be good presents for our families, but also because we felt a bit sorry for them waiting all day for perhaps the one or two boats that would come here to look at the ruins.

5
Iñak Uyu – Court of Women

The entire island of Isla de la Luna is considered an important religious site. The ruins we visited, called *Iñak Uyu* (court of women), were the remains of a spiritual center for women. The ruins were well-preserved with a simplicity that I found very comforting. The main building was divided into four units with four small doorways that looked like they would fit stylishly in any Santa Fe, New Mexico neighborhood. Each doorway was small and framed by a pyramid

Iñak Uyu doorway

of cut bricks. Two windows framed each building at the top. What intrigued Justin and I was that behind the doors there didn't appear to be space for a room, It was as if the doorways were for strictly aesthetic purposes, or maybe people just stood in the doorways for ceremonial reasons. Or, perhaps they were rooms to store corn and thus didn't have to be very big. In the silence that surrounded us as we walked around this special place, it was nice to have so many secrets hidden in these ancient walls where people like us could ponder what might have been.

What I found most attractive about this site was the way the sun-bleached mud buildings were designed to fit so perfectly into the surrounding brown hillside. These buildings appeared to be

Iñak Uyu fitting into landscape

built for function rather than for grandness. The big pyramids and giant tributes to kings and leaders that we associate with so many Latin American ruins, although structurally impressive, are a bit pompous to me, and I am almost happy to see them in ruins or gobbled up by forests. People like me would have never been allowed to come close to these kinds of places unless we were being put into labor. It took the sweat and beatings of countless laborers to create many of the world's ancient spiritual edifices. This place felt much different. It seemed to be a very humble place, serenely beautiful and peaceful. And there was nobody else around, although we did see the remains of the "Pachamama" ritual – a circle of rocks with some burned wood in the center – from the night before. Perhaps we had missed an interesting ceremony, but we felt no regrets standing next to these humble yet fascinating ruins all by ourselves in the peaceful sun.

Also fascinating was a stone wall, still intact, that showcased incredible Incan masonry. Here was a wall made out of rectangular stones, cut precisely and without the use of mortar, fitting so perfectly that you could not slip a piece of paper between stones. We stood in awe of the incredible precision and knowledge of the builders that allowed this stone wall to stand upright for so many years without the use of adhesive mortar. There were hundreds of rocks sitting seamlessly together. This was a beautiful example of human craft and artistry.

Incan masonry

The Journey Home

1
Back to the Mainland

After our visit to Iñak Uyu, we headed back to camp, had lunch, and after a rest, decided to go across the lake to the mainland where we saw some inviting beaches in the distance. We felt as if we had explored Isla de la Luna enough, and as the backside of the island did not have any good camping beaches, we felt that it was time to move on. Crossing over to the mainland would take us to our last camping spot before we would head back to Copacabana and the "city life."

It was strange to think that this would be our last day camping out since we had really fallen into a comfortable routine together. The novelty of kayak camping had worn off and we just felt that this was the normal way to be. I loved it. I loved going to bed at sunset. I loved the transition from freezing to warm after jumping in my mummy sleeping bag. I loved waking up at sunset to the peaceful lapping of Lake Titicaca close to our tents, and the slow mornings of long peaceful breakfasts in the warm sun. Seeing our families again would be wonderful, but long peaceful mornings would soon be a thing of the past! We packed up our gear, said our last goodbyes to Isla de la Luna, with its beaches of grazing llamas, laughing children and beautiful ruins (still in use!).

The coastline we were headed towards looked so much bigger; the vista held so much more land than the end-points we had been paddling towards in the past week or so on the islands. We were headed to a landmass that reached all the way to our homes in California. Getting closer, we saw what looked like an ideal beach for camping with plenty of trees and sand and even a few caves surrounded by the always-visible agricultural terraces. I didn't feel the need to seek out sirenando caves anymore. I had already received my sirena song, so the caves we saw would remain charango-less, at least while *we* were camping there.

We arrived with plenty of time to set up camp and explore a bit. The beach had a strange feeling to it, perhaps because it was attached to the mainland and, therefore, more accessible. There was obvious use by locals, such as nearby piles of plants that had been harvested. We couldn't figure out what these long-leafed plants were but speculated they might be for weaving. We couldn't see a trail to any village, so we didn't know if we were on somebody's property or not. Not surprisingly, there were more trees here than on any place we had visited on the islands. The rugged topography of the islands and the reality of limited resources over hundreds of years had left the islands virtually deforested.

As the sun began to set, the beach was covered with strange and spooky-shaped shadows created by the gnarled trees. As the night darkened, what started out like a sweet little beach took on an almost sinister look that was accentuated by a strange and large unidentifiable nocturnal bird making bizarre croaking noises as it passed overhead. We also heard fireworks from nearby towns as celebrations continued on this last day of the *Coronación de La Virgen de Copacabana* holiday. Perhaps it was because the trip was coming to a close, and we were mentally and physically distancing ourselves from the lake – our minds already returning home to our loved ones – but I hadn't felt so uncomfortable and out of my element than I did on this beach that night. It felt very different to be camping on the mainland, which seemed tethered to the realities of the world, whereas on the island we had felt adrift from the continent in a realm of timelessness. Here we could jump into someone's pickup truck and be at an internet café within an hour.

Throughout the night, the wind whipped around and the trees made strange noises which overwhelmed the usual sounds of tiny waves crashing on the shores. My imagination ran wild with the new sounds. Since we were close to a town, perhaps the now drunken festival-goers were heading to the beach and wondering what the people in the two tents were up to? I have been to various festivals around the world filled with much "merriment" which sometimes tilts into drunkenness and crusty encounters with locals. It was amazing to think of the difference in feeling of camping on the islands compared to this mainland beach where all of a sudden anything could happen. I had a fitful sleep, to say the least, and more intense longings for returning home.

We awoke to a calm morning as always (we weren't attacked overnight, thank God) and as I knew this was our last camp out on the lake, I walked over to the edge of the beach with my charango and gave a "Thank You" concert. The only thing that felt worthy and right was to play my sirena song over and over again as the sun warmed the rocks. I was so grateful that I was given this song that seemed to be just as much a part of this lake as the sun, the island, and the strange trees that surrounded me. This trip gave me a most amazing gift: a musical memory that came from the ecology of this lake. Music…as integral a part of the surroundings as the wind, rock and water. My song was a lake song, a Sonia song, a charango song, a trip song. A siren song. I was grateful.

2
Return to Copacabana

We headed back to Copacabana anticipating an empty town with a hung-over atmosphere as the *Coronación de la Virgen de Copacabana* was supposedly over. We could unload our boats in peace as the locals nursed themselves back to life with mug after mug of coca leaf tea. After a four-hour paddle, we passed by the Bolivian naval station just outside of Copacabana. Just as we were commenting on

Returning to Copacabana

the absurdity of a navy on this lake, we heard a commanding voice from a loud speaker at the station shout, "*PARA POR FAVOR.*" "STOP, PLEASE!" Because we were tired and didn't want anything to do with the Bolivian Navy, we kept paddling, feigning deafness, hoping they would not come after us. I had quick Hollywood-influenced images of interrogations held in dank concrete cells with mustached colonels burning cigarettes into our arms as they questioned us while simultaneously planting drugs in our boat. We kept paddling, looking straight ahead, praying to the sirenas of the lake to protect us. Nobody followed us, thank goodness. We provided the excitement of the morning on this tranquil day, but thankfully the Bolivian Navy had backed down from this confrontation – our own Cuban missile crisis. We paddled onward to a hot shower, clean clothes and food without raw potatoes and onions in it.

3
Strange Water

Our first question upon pulling up to the shore of Copacabana was why the water was so brown and murky? The casualties of the previous day's festivities, men and women lying down on the road and beach, bottles of liquor strewn about, soon gave us the brutal truth. The water had been an open latrine for the last few days, and we had to forge through the muck to disembark from our vessel. This was going to take some strategic maneuvering. A few still-standing partiers gathered to watch the gringos try to land their tiny boat. We struggled to get close to the beach so as to have as little body contact with the polluted water as possible. There were little wooden docks along the beach, but these were filled with other people's boats and colorful quilted bags filled with who-knows-what. There didn't appear to be any room for our kayak to dock, so as we inched closer to shore, I jumped out of the boat

Aftermath of the Coronación de La Virgen de Copacabana

hoping for the best. The water's smell was potent, the brown color extremely unappealing, and our first bodily contact with the water was distressing. The water was not cold as I had anticipated, as it had been throughout our trip – it was warmish. Yuck! Now we had to get our stuff out of the boat without letting it touch the warm stuff (I hesitate to call it water anymore). Twenty minutes later, we had a pile of gear in the street, unfortunately about as unhygienic as the water – a fetid pile of sweaty, sandy, oniony, garishly-colored camping gear. Our feet were mucking through the water the entire time, and when we were through, I just wanted to saw off my contaminated feet. We took turns carrying our possessions back to our hotel where we could take a warm shower and scrape off our toxic outer layers. Our kayak trip was officially over.

4
Last Night in the Copa

Back in civilization, washed and ready to celebrate, we set out for the most elusive of all food, the *trucha*! We walked down the strangely subdued streets of Copacabana (if only the walls could speak of the last few days of fiesta revelry!) looking for a place to eat. As we walked by the home/restaurant of the friendly people we had met before our paddle trip, we greeted them and told them a few details of our trip. I think they were surprised that we had actually been gone for so long as it was not something they would consider doing. Visiting the islands was a day trip for them, not a ten-day expedition. I felt strangely protective of my sirena story, so I didn't bring it up.

Hanging on the wall in the restaurant was a painting of the islands, which I had noticed when we had eaten there before. It was a simple picture but more defined than our map, capturing the entirety of our kayak route. I asked the owner if the artist who made that painting lived in town, and he said he knew someone who could paint a replica for us. I thought that was the end of it, because we would be leaving the next day, surely not enough time to have someone paint me a picture. He told me not to worry, that the painting would be ready for us in the morning. He would go to the artist's house right then. I paid him some money in advance and with a smile he headed off to order me a painting, which seemed about as simple as ordering a pizza. With astonished grins on our faces, we headed out again to get some trucha.

The restaurant was an interesting choice from the start as it was the most romantic spot in town. It was half-filled with loving couples squeezed next to each other around dimly lit tiny tables or snuggling in secluded booths. We had washed up a bit but we still probably looked a little feral, and, though Justin and I were much closer to each other than we had been before the trip, romance was still out of the question. Besides we had a date with a trucha. As always, a list of ways to prepare the trucha was presented on the menu, and there was one in particular that looked simple and appetizing, trucha with a "light orange glaze." I asked if flour was an ingredient (*harina de trigo*) and the young waiter assured me it wasn't. Yes, finally, after two and a half weeks there would be the famous taste of Titicaca trucha in my belly! As we sat with our grown-out beards, sun and wind-burned faces taut from paddling muscles, we felt like quite the rugged adventurers. I love this feeling after a trip where one's body is pushed to its limits, feeling anything but tired. It actually felt like a return to our "normal" physical state. We had some Chilean red wine to celebrate and to toast our luck. "Clink" went the glasses and, as if on cue, out came our truchas, mine covered in orange glaze over a deeply battered fish. Damn.

As we sat (Justin eating and me watching him eat), a musician came in to play as his friend passed around a hat for money. He was uniquely terrible, with guitar strings and vocal chords tuned to different scales. Whatever romantic mood had been created by the candles and small tables was washed away with each disastrous attempt at music-making. I felt sorry for the ragamuffin musician, as I have been in his position before although with more musicality, I hope.

I performed with a quartet of musicians for a year, playing at a Mexican restaurant every Friday night. Our job was to go from table to table and play a song for the diners. The restaurant was already small and four musicians playing loud folk music and crowding into your personal eating space made it truly claustrophobic for everyone. We played with practiced smiles as they listened with polite mock-enthusiasm, neither party really enjoying the musical experience.

5
Bus Ride home and Almost Killing Someone

The next morning we had breakfast at our hotel and got our belongings ready for the trip home. I walked over to our friend's place to see if my painting was ready and lo and behold, it was! It was an exact replica of the one on his wall. I asked if it was the same artist and he said it was not, which was remarkable because they were identical. Perhaps all the local artists had the same template, a sort of paint by the numbers art for tourists like me. Well, I am not an art critic, and I loved my painting.

Waiting for the bus to La Paz

We got our gear to the plaza where all of the buses were leaving and booked a passage back to La Paz. I wish I could say that exiting Copacabana was uneventful, but this would not be true. When we were ready to load up the bus, the driver motioned for us to load our bags on to the roof, and he climbed up so we could hand them to him. Justin told him that the boats were very, very heavy, and he grunted, *"Sí sí"* (as in, you don't know how strong I am, skinny kid) and as I turned around to buy some peanuts for the trip, I heard a crash and a thump. The crash was one of our bags falling off the bus and the thump was the result of our bag landing on a very small elderly Bolivian woman! There was a vacuous silence as we all watched for the twitching of life in the tiny body that was smashed underneath our cargo. I could see the accusations of murder bubbling up in the people gathered around us. Then, miracle of miracles, she slowly rolled out from beneath the bags, brushed herself off and smiled a toothless grin. We hadn't killed anyone on our trip, hooray! I wanted to hug and kiss her but didn't want to draw any more attention to ourselves, so we just apologized profusely. I even gave her our bag of peanuts, gentleman that I am. When we got on the bus, she smiled at us. What a tough old lady!

As we headed out of Copacabana, I was filled with emotion. A dream had come true for me, which is not something to be taken lightly. The earth had sung to me, and I was able to take off enough layers of myself to hear the song. As we took the five-hour bus ride back to La Paz, I composed in my little journal what I entitled "The Siren's Call."

The Siren's Call

Siren songs are out there. Perhaps disguised as the wind, a bird's song, the murmur of a river, the crashing of a wave, or sung from the lips of a mermaid herself, these songs are meant for us to hear. The problem is that all too often, we humans have a hard time hearing them. We have surrounded ourselves with a soundtrack that covers up so much of what is important to hear from our natural landscape. We listen to our cell phones and I-pods, our homes are filled with televisions and appliances. We walk to our cars in the morning to the sound of leaf-blowers and garbage trucks. People who hear the siren songs are often the children, the spiritual leaders, or the "crazy" people unafraid to listen to the more subtle music, whose tones and frequencies remain hidden for the unadventurous. These songs provide for deeper understanding of our relationship to the natural world and it is to our peril if we don't start listening.

Once we are lucky enough to hear the siren's song, we shouldn't follow the path of ancient mariners blindly crashing upon the rocks, as their desires came from trying to somehow capture this intoxicating beauty for themselves. The song cannot be understood through the ears of ego and ownership, because this song is not directed to any one person but to everyone and everything. The song is meant for us to experience and join in on the melody. The song should seduce our best and most creative self to move forward, past the battlegrounds and rocky points that prohibit us from feeling alive and filled with love and compassion. **The siren song is not sung for us, it is sung through us. It is not sung for one, but for everyone. When you finally hear the siren's call it isn't for you at all.**

City Sirenas

1
Looking for a Siren Song in the City

Back in La Paz, we had an extra day for shopping before we headed back to California. My initial intention was to buy a new high quality charango to take home along with the one I used on the kayak trip. However, by this time I considered the charango I had used for sirenando to be wonderful-sounding, magical even. I didn't want to turn it into a trip artifact, a souvenir from the trip to be displayed alongside woven blankets and figurines. This charango had earned its right to be played. Now the issue became which charango would be my main one when I got home. What would my hierarchy of charangos be now? It could be tricky.

I sometimes find myself oddly trying not to hurt my instrument's feelings. Instruments are such vehicles for creativity, I find myself attributing human qualities to them, not only creative ones such as soulful and melancholic, but also attributes like jealousy. I have various charangos at home, but I primarily play just one of them. On the rare occasion that I do take out another one – when I want a specific-sounding charango for recording in the studio, I find myself feeling guilty for leaving my main charango behind. I wonder if it's feelings will be hurt and if it will sound "wounded" the next time I play it. Ridiculous? Think of all the famous musicians who give names to their mainstay instruments. I remember looking at Willie Nelson's guitar all battered with holes and discolorations and thinking that they both had gone through a lot together, almost like a long marriage. I have played my charango so much it has become discolored not only from years of sweat but also from bleeding fingers, a result of many multiple hour jam sessions and performances.

Musicians often refuse to let other people play their instruments as other people's "energy" might pollute the instrument's sound. I remember touching a percussionist's conga drum at a musical camp and having him scream at me for putting my "hand grease" on his drum. His point – which he so eloquently yelled at me – was that his drum's sound and tone had come from years of his sweat blending into the skin of his drum. His skin and the cow skin covering the conga drum had become one skin. I slithered away from the irate drummer and learned an important lesson about the strong relationship between musicians and their instruments.

As my charango search seemed to be over, I decided instead to search for a person extremely important to the charango-playing world, Ernesto Cavour, the "father" of the Bolivian charango. I had heard of this man when I first picked up a charango in La Paz in 1992 because all of the "how to" books and chord charts were written by him. Every music store had his books, CDs, and workbooks, and I duly bought them to teach myself how to play this beautiful instrument. His books were filled with pictures, stories and history of the charango, and you could tell that for this man, charangos were his life. I soon learned that his books and audio-cassettes were distributed throughout the world, and he was a leading authority on Andean music in general. I knew he lived in La Paz, and I was also told that he had a wonderful charango museum that was well worth a visit.

Wall of charangos

Justin and I decided to head out to the museum in a taxi and soon found ourselves in a very quaint part of the city with cobblestone streets and colorful artist galleries and cafes. The museum was situated on a small street, with nothing to identify it but a barely visible placard that significantly had a picture of a mermaid strumming a tiny guitar. I felt like a four-year old entering Disneyland for the first time as I passed beneath the sirena's gaze into a courtyard with staircases on all four sides leading to rooms filled with charangos and other Andean instruments. It was an amazing place with dozens of charangos displayed on walls with accompanying photographs of *charanguistas* of the past 100 years. There were also crazy charango inventions by the curator Ernesto Cavour. These included charangos in the shape of hearts, with double and triple necks, with panpipes built into them, and of course numerous ones made from the armored shells of armadillos. It was a charango paradise, and clearly a labor of intense love from its architect Cavour. There was also an interactive section with drums, marimbas and other musical creations; a wall with various posters of Cavour's concerts from around the world; and display cases with antique instruments made from condor bones, totora reeds and llama skins, representing music that has been played in Bolivia for hundreds of years. It was a marvelous museum, unpretentious, accessible and incredibly rich.

As there didn't appear to be any museum guards, I approached one of the young, smiling music students who were studying at the museum and asked if Ernesto Cavour ever visited there. She said that, in fact, he was supposed to be visiting later that afternoon. What incredible luck! My heart jumped with the possibility of a chance to meet this man so dedicated to the charango. Seeing the picture of the mermaid playing the charango-like instrument at the entrance to the museum gave me an extra incentive to try and talk to him about my experience on Isla del Sol. Hopefully, I would gain more insights into the connection of sirens and charangos in the Andes. I was certain he had a wealth of such stories and hoped he would have the time to share some.

Because it was still early in the day and there were still some things we wanted to do before leaving the next day for the U.S., we decided to head back to the hotel before Cavour's arrival. As we left the museum, we passed by a table with a few charangos on it and since they weren't with the rest of the ones on display, I asked a person behind the table if I could look at, and perhaps play them.

She said that I could, and that they were actually some of Señor Cavour's charangos and were for sale. For sale! It was like being told that I could buy one of Segovia's guitars! My hands immediately began to sweat as I picked up one of the charangos. Both were made with the armadillo back, and seemed to be well played with nicks, indentations, and discolorations on the wood, all created from Mr. Cavour's expert hands. The first charango sounded fine but took a while to get in tune. It had a quiet tone, and the tuning pegs were slightly bent which made tuning difficult, but it was still played by the master so I held it with reverence. The second charango was a smaller model, sometimes called *walaycho*, and as I did not own this size charango I was instantly intrigued. I picked up the tiny charango about twenty inches long and strummed it. My God, it was in perfect tune and strummed so softly and smoothly, it felt as if I were strumming silken strings. The sound was clear and pure, celestial-like. I fell in love with it. It was a gorgeous instrument made of dark wood, well-used over many years of play and the armadillo back was worn but in excellent condition. It was no ordinary instrument and I desired it immensely.

As this was a well-used charango, I began to imagine Ernesto playing it. Had he placed it by a *huaca* somewhere in the highlands, and had a sirena perhaps played it? I felt this was a once in lifetime opportunity to have such a special instrument, so with trepidation I asked if I could buy the charango. The young woman said that she thought this particular instrument was possibly sold to a man who lived outside of La Paz, but if he didn't call or come by the museum later that day, perhaps I could buy it. This seemed vague and troubling. I wanted to buy it right then! Who was this man to take away my newfound love? Perhaps we could duel for the rights to play it. She looked at my troubled face and with sympathy told me to come back later. I was intending to do that anyway because I wanted to meet Ernesto Cavour. Perhaps there was still a chance I could take this instrument home with me. So with great regret

I left the beautiful *walaycho-charango* on the table and left the museum with Justin.

Before we headed back to our hotel, Justin decided to get a shave and a haircut at a local barber. He picked an old-fashioned-looking place and asked if the barber shaved beards as well as cut hair. He said he did. Justin actually shaves his head to a stubble, so basically he was asking for a whole head shave. As the man took out his straight-edged shaver, I left to find a cup of tea. As I walked away leaving Justin in the hands of the man with a long razor, I looked with concern at his poor sunburned face, his lips so chapped that I actually feared they might be permanently damaged. I wondered what the barber was thinking of him as well.

After my tea I went back to pick up Justin, and there he was, freshly-shaved and toweled dry, looking much less scruffy, but unfortunately with no improvement to his lip region. His story of the shaving session was macabre and comical. Every time the man asked a question, the sharp menacing shaving blade would wave dangerously close to essential parts of Justin's head. Justin would reply trying not to move an inch lest the blade nick him in the artery, or take off an ear. He also noticed that his lips had opened as he was talking and blood was flowing onto his teeth. Both people involved with the shaving process were terrified of the other in what was looking like a scene from a Quentin Tarantino movie. I couldn't stop laughing at the image. Justin didn't find it as amusing.

Back at the hotel we went off on our separate ways. Justin was looking for some last-minute souvenirs for his family and I wanted to buy some charango strings which are difficult to find in the U.S. I had a hard time waiting for my return to the museum and kept wondering if the charango was being sold at that moment. I felt a range of emotions from jealousy to greed to hopefulness. When I couldn't wait any longer, I headed back to the Charango Museum to discover my fate while Justin rested in the hotel.

I passed beneath the museum's sign with the sirena and headed straight for the counter where the charangos were for sale. I met with the same young lady who had been there before and asked if the gentleman had picked up the charango, or if (please, oh please) he had decided not to buy it. As I could not see it on the counter, I feared the worst. She looked at me with intense relief saying that she had been completely mistaken about the charango and that it actually was never for sale at all. It belonged to one of the music students. When he heard that it was almost sold, he became quite distraught. I could see why! It was a remarkable charango and I would have been devastated to lose it too. The man from outside of La Paz was buying the other charango, the one that had not impressed me as much. He had called and was going to pick it up the next day. I felt sad to not be able to own that special charango, but also relieved to not have caused any grief to a fellow musician.

I moved on to my second dream – to get to meet Ernesto Cavour in person. The lady said he usually showed up after 4:00 p.m., so I went next door to wait and have another *coca* tea. He finally showed up close to 5:00 p.m., having an intense conversation with a Japanese man in a business suit. It looked like some important international cultural negotiation was going on and there I was in my camping clothes looking awestruck. I quickly sat close by and waited to see if I would have an opportunity to talk with him. I had bought one of his books at the museum that I hoped he would sign, which I also hoped would work as an ice-breaker to further conversation.

The opportunity finally arrived. As he concluded his conversation with the other man, I walked up to him and asked if he could autograph my book. As he signed the book, I told him I had been fascinated with charangos for many years and that I found his museum to be an amazing resource. I then threw caution to the wind and told him of my experience on Isla del Sol looking for evidence of sirenas playing charangos. I blurted out that I was a charango player myself and that I had an interesting experience in a small cave on Isla Del Sol. Deciding to put all the cards on the table, I told him that I believed a sirena had played my charango. Then I waited uncomfortably for his response.

The silent look he gave me could have meant two things. One, I was another loopy tourist who had heard about sirens and charangos and he was not about to confide in me about his beliefs or non-beliefs in the matter; or, his quiet look was a silent recognition of a fellow believer and lucky recipient of the siren's musical gift. I hoped it was the latter. After this brief silent gaze, he smiled at me, gave me back my autographed book and said, "*Sigue tocando, amigo*" (keep playing, friend), touched my shoulder with his calloused charango-playing hands, and without another word headed up the stairs of his wonderful Willy Wonka-like museum.

I decided to walk home to the hotel after this emotional day, my last one in Bolivia, soaking in the wonderful strangeness of this high elevation city. As I headed out of the neighborhood where the museum stood, I heard the unmistakable strums of a charango, celestial notes floating towards the snowy peaks surrounding the city. Beautiful Bolivia!

2
Airport Adventure

The next day Justin and I woke up to the sound of gunshots. We went out to the hall lobby, and the attendants calmly stated that it was just another strike. The gunshots didn't seem to faze them, but it made us very nervous. We decided to brave a look outside and could see people in the street in front of the hotel heading towards the main boulevard where thousands of people were marching. We soon found out it was a teacher's strike (with guns!) and that they were blocking many of the main roads, including the one to the airport. Crap. Now, I am all for teachers getting what they deserve, but we needed to get home! We were leaving that night and had to be at the airport by 5:30 p.m., so we hoped that the strike would end by then. When we mentioned this to the hotel workers, they laughed lightheartedly and said it could last for days but not to worry, La Paz taxi drivers had their own special routes, and we would make it to the airport somehow.

Somewhat encouraged, we ventured out again to witness the striking teachers. Women and men paraded through the streets with signs asking for the dismissal of an education minister who was not addressing the needs of the teachers' union. Bolivia is known for its vociferous protests, justified by hundreds of years of inequalities. Protests in Cochabamba, Bolivia made international headlines in 2000 in what has been called the *Guerra del Agua* (Water War).

In the "Water War," the people of Cochabamba wanted to have unrestrained access to their water sources, which clashed with the claims of Agua del Tunari, a multinational water agency, which wanted to be the region's supplier of water with exclusive rights to the municipal water network. The company wanted citizens to stop their own unregulated water collecting, and so the agency installed water meters on wells to accurately quantify water usage and charge customers accordingly. In a country where minimum wage is less than seventy dollars a month, water bills were taking up a large portion of people's monthly income. Many citizens could not pay their water bill and thus were in effect excluded from their water sources.

Besides the financial inequity, some people of the region maintained that their water rights and their connection to their water sources were human cultural/spiritual rights. They questioned how regional water sources could be "owned" and regulated by outside forces such as multinational companies and private enterprises with no cultural connection to the watershed. These protestors proclaimed that no one could own water because water is a part of who they are. Water rights are human rights. A region's water is the lifeblood of it's culture, manifest in the agriculture, the structures of towns and village, and, as I have learned, in the sirena songs of the charango players.

The protests lasted for months and gained international attention as Bolivians blockaded major roads with thousands of protestors flooding the streets. The Bolivian government finally cancelled the contract with Aguas del Turani, but unfortunately many people were injured and lives were even lost during the protests.

The teacher protest was much more peaceful, the early morning gunfire not withstanding, but showed no sign of ending on our day of departure. Justin talked to a man on the street about the protest and he said the reason they were protesting was because they could. Meaning, under their current government headed by the popular president Evo Morales, people felt more able to voice their opinion without intervention and intimidation from government forces. It was safer to protest, so they felt more comfortable doing so. And protest they did, throughout the day, as our flight departure time fast approached.

We checked out of our rooms early with our gear all packed and asked the hotel people to get us a taxi to the airport which was located in El Alto, the ridge top city where many of the poorest people of the area live. On a normal day it was probably a half hour ride to the airport, but today we had no idea how long it would take us, so we gave ourselves close to two hours. Plenty of time, we thought.

The taxi promptly arrived with a cab driver who, with a solemn expression, told us he would be able to get us to the airport by 5:30, and that he had a way of bypassing the protests and blockades. We headed out of La Paz, passing though narrow alleyways and steep roads with deep potholes and crumbling sidewalks. Justin insightfully commented that many of the businesses seemed to be car related. Street after street of tire shops, engines hanging from chains and men in blue suits with grease streaks on their faces. The roads were treacherous, and we could see why the car mechanics were so necessary.

Having driven on many Latin American roads that were in bad condition, and in taxicabs where the driver drove too fast with little regard for pedestrians, bicycles or basically anything in his way, it was alarming to feel that there were indeed higher levels of driving stress to be had. This was a world-class tourist "scarer!!" We felt unsafe and had a sinking feeling that we were lost. As the roads continued to deteriorate, Justin took on an increasingly worried look and I was also sweating bullets. Justin said something very understated, but so poetically pure and to the point, "This doesn't look good to me." I agreed that it didn't. The solemn appearance on the cab driver's face changed to something more deranged and we began to wonder if perhaps he was taking us to a closed off street where his cohorts would rob us, or possibly worse. Visions from all of the most frightening traveler movies (*Midnight Express*) and crazy-people movies (*Silence of the Lambs*) began to flood my brain. Justin repeated his sage sentence, "This does not look good to me." Again, I found his sentiments right on the mark.

As the sun began to set and meeting our arrival time at the airport began to seem less and less probable, the surroundings began to look even more surreal. Children and pigs played in the streets, drunks lay next to *abueletas* in colorful *polleras* who stirred steaming pots of what could have been food – or some kind of Andean witchcraft. The air was red-tinged, and steam rose from manhole covers. It looked post-apocalyptic, and we sat in the back seat of the taxi with our hearts in our throats. Was this the end? We sat speechless as we watched a small naked boy defecating in the street with a mongrel dog waiting patiently to feast on the feces as it was exiting the boy's body. I tell you it was Hieronymus Bosch out there!

Just when it appeared that we were destined to miss our flight home, we turned down a street and we were at the entrance to the airport. Our drive through purgatory was over. The driver turned around and with the same smile-less face grunted, *"Llegamos."* We're here. I just wanted to hug him now as all traces of distrust vanished into the cool, well-lit, un-apocalyptic airport air.

We dragged our gear into the airport with the help of two porters who we had specifically asked not to help us as we didn't have the money to pay them. Searching through pockets and backpacks, we were finally able to scrounge together a few coins, which they accepted with great contempt as if we were the lowest of the lows. Stingy cheating ingrates! They left muttering what we could only guess were Aymara insults.

Inside the airport it was turmoil due to a just-announced global requirement that no one was allowed on the plane with any kind of liquid container. There had been a high level terrorist plot to blow up a plane by detonating some kind of explosive from a plastic water bottle. Arguments and debates rang out with people pleading to keep their contact lens solution or other medical liquid, which were all unceremoniously dumped inside of a big white plastic bag. It all seemed a bit heavy-handed. We saw chapstick containers, mouthwash and even our water bottles (which had made it through two weeks of paddling) disappear into the white bag.

How ironic that, in our last hours in Bolivia, I held a charango filled to the brim with musical energy from Lake Titicaca's water, as I watched airport authorities considering water a place to hide terrorist's anger. With these new requirements, our flights were delayed, so we just sat and waited and dreamed about the open arms of our families.

The Song On and On

1
Taking the Siren Song Home

A few weeks after a wonderful airport reunion and time at home finishing up a room for our soon-to-be-born baby, Gwynne began her labor. We spent a relatively gentle morning at home, and after walking to the park on that beautiful late-summer day, we decided it was time to go to the birthing center to have Sonia. The pregnancy was coming to an end, and we were excited to welcome Sonia into our family. At the hospital, we were ushered into a beautiful spacious room with a bathtub and a comfortable-looking bed for delivering our baby. This was such a different environment from the days of stirrups and stainless steel when I was brought into the world. Gwynne's mom was on her way to the hospital and our boy was at a friend's house waiting for his sister.

Everything was as smooth as it could be, until Gwynne decided to take a warm bath to ease the contractions that were getting quite strong. Once in the bathroom, her water broke and she felt "a little funny." I could see in her face that she knew something was wrong and that whatever it took, she wanted to get the baby out safely. They brought her back to the bed and placed monitors on her and felt inside her to see how the baby was doing. The fetal heart monitor reading was decreasing dangerously during contractions. The midwife had a look of concern on her face as she felt something inside the birth canal. It was the umbilical cord piled up at the entrance where the baby's head should be. She pulled out her hand, and immediately the heart rate of the baby plummeted. The midwife put her hand immediately back in the womb, and the heart rate went back up. With her hand in the birth canal she was able to prevent the baby's head from pushing out. This in turn prevented the head from squeezing the umbilical cord that gave oxygen to our baby. She said that she was not going to take her hand out again as Gwynne, with every ounce of her soul, shouted "Please don't!!!" She got a nurse to call the emergency crew, and then everything became very tense. With her hand still pushing Sonia back into the birth canal, the midwife actually laid down with Gwynne on the hospital gurney while some nurses carted Gwynne out of our peaceful room and into the halls leading to emergency surgery. I barely had enough time to squeeze her hand. I was in shock. Gwynne's mom appeared outside the room with a white face. She knew we were in emergency mode. I wanted my wife safe and my baby saved. We have friends who have lost their babies during birth and I couldn't bear the thought. I paced up and down the hall for a while, as nurses and surgeons fled past on the way to the emergency surgery room.

My adrenaline was pounding so hard I started to feel queasy. I sat down and realized that I had to put all of my positive energy into the room next door where my wife and baby were battling for life. Praying seemed like a good idea but since I don't pray often, the idea felt foreign to me. So I started humming *Sonia's Song*. The song's intensity came back to me immediately, and the rhythmic memories of wind on water, the song of the *sirena* filled up my mind and heart. The song's repetitious melody became a mantra, which I sang over and over quietly in my head. Visions of a healthy daughter and smiling wife colored the musical notes with hope. I sang over and over, staring straight at the floor, trying to recall visions of the lake and the special beach where my sirena song was first played. I tried to blot out the fact that I was in a hospital with my wife in an emergency room.

I don't know how long I had been quietly singing *Sonia's Song* when a doctor with surgical greens and mask walked out of the surgery room where my wife had the emergency c-section, and my heart leapt. Was it good or bad news? He handed me a bundle of sheets and inside was the most beautiful face staring right into my eyes. No crying, just the most deep dark brown eyes (the only ones in our family!) alert and so healthy.

"Your wife is doing fine and the baby is perfect," he said to me. And she WAS perfect. I was so grateful my legs almost buckled. Gwynne's mom came over for a look, and she started crying. Here she was, our Sonia. Brought into the world by a strong heroic mother, the prayers of a grandmother, and the siren song from a lake far, far, away.

2
Taking the *Sirena* to Work

My day-to-day job is performing musical shows with my wife about environmental themes to children and their families. Our group is called ZunZun, which is named after a type of hummingbird in Cuba. Our specialty is programs about water issues such as water conservation, storm drain run-off and clean watersheds. We have been doing these programs for many years and perform for over 100,000 people a year in schools and festivals. As part of our show, I now include the story of how charangos can capture the sound of water spirits in the Andes. In Christian schools I tend to say, "The sounds of water enter the charango," rather than spirits, so as not to risk being driven out of the school for instigating pagan beliefs into the student body. But whatever the words, when I tell the students to listen to the sounds of water as I play the charango, they are spellbound, as quiet as a group of 200-400 children, ages six to twelve, could possibly be. This is not due to my charango-playing technique or expertise, but the amazing sonic quality of this instrument, which produces the sounds of moving water like no other instrument I can think of.

In our shows, we also try to get students to move their bodies as much as possible to our "water music." We remind them that like our planet Earth, water makes up about 67% of our bodies. We are more fluid than solid! In class, students are asked to sit up straight in their chairs, pay attention, and not move too much. In our shows we immediately invite students to move their water bodies, activating muscle memories of swimming in the ocean, running through sprinklers or floating quietly in a swimming pool. All around us water is constantly moving (dancing) around in creeks, rivers, underground aquifers, evaporation and rain, and these are movements we can also incorporate into our own water bodies. Ask most students to move like a wave and they know exactly what to do. To loosen up the shy and "too cool" students, we always model this freedom of movement (dancing) ourselves. We have found that watching teachers, principals and our tired old bodies dance around is quite humorous (and at times perhaps scary) to most kids, and it motivates them to try as well. How could they look any more ridiculous than we do! To get people to care for their surroundings and develop an environmental ethic, I strongly believe we should not just feed facts and figures into our brain, but engage the whole body. Music and dance are wonderful mediums for achieving this.

While working in environmental education in various countries in Latin America, I was always discouraged to see that environmental education was taught for the most part with workbooks and pamphlets written outside of the country (mostly from the U.S.) with dry terse writing, unattractively presented. There was little to inspire the teachers and students who were to use them. I walked into many classrooms and saw these materials sitting unused in bookshelves. This is shameful because with most cultures there is an incredibly rich medium for environmental education through the arts, dance, music, poetry and theater that is not being tapped. I always find it rewarding to create an appreciation of environmental issues using the cultural richness available in a community. In Costa Rica, I worked with teachers to create plays and dances about the sea turtle which the children performed for their families on the beaches during the sea turtle migration season. Watching the "Birth of a Sea Turtle" dance by five and six year old kids in front of their parents (some of whom were turtle egg poachers) on a tropical beach, where later that night turtles would arrive to lay their eggs, inspired everyone there to understand the importance of a healthy, unpolluted beach, not only for the sea turtles, but for the people as well.

As a global community, we are becoming increasingly aware of the degradation of our planet. We are given factual information; statistics, graphs and projections of the environmental disasters that await us in the future. All of this information is essential, but to activate our hearts and minds together we must engage all parts of ourselves. I have watched my twelve-year old son become overwhelmed by the apocalyptic rhetoric of the state of the planet, which must be the case for many other children around the world.

Now is the time for artists to inspire hope and action to meet these problems. Now is the time for siren songs.

After my trip to Bolivia, I returned to performing water shows with the sirena song singing inside of me. I realized that the siren's job was now my job. I must try my hardest to turn water into music. All my years of surfing, kayaking, bodysurfing and immersing myself in water must now be brought into focus to inspire and entertain others to embrace and celebrate their connection to their water bodies and to their planet. When we hear the siren's song, we are listening to the water inside us, and the water that surrounds us. We are listening to the song of all life on Earth – the flowers, the mountains, the fish and the worms. We are listening to a beautiful intoxicating sound that gives us hope and the knowledge that we must take care of our Earth and celebrate its beauty.

Ever since my experience with the creation of Sonia's song, my charango has seemed touched by the gods of music. Maybe it was just the memories of that special night on the beach, but I can still feel the magic in the string and wood. This charango...and its player will never be the same.

The Siren's guitar

For more information about the author's musical group ZunZun, and to purchase their music, visit:

zunzuntunes.com

More books from River Sanctuary Publishing...

A Moment in Time Book One and Two, a memoir by Steve D. Wilson, 2011. $16.95

Affirmations for Everyday Living: Create more clarity, success, and joy in your life, by Annie Elizabeth, 2010. $17.95

Banana Slug of the Santa Cruz Mountains: Up Close and Personal Encounters of Fact, Fiction, and Fun, by Gary Bartos. Full color. $14.95

The Unorthodox Life: Walking Your Own Path to the Divine, by Kathy McCall, 2009. $15.95

Notes to Self: Meditations on Being, by Christy Deena, 2011. $15.95

Wild Joy: Ruminations, poetry by Paul Goldman. $12.00

River Sanctuary Publishing
P.O. Box 1561
Felton, California 95018
www.riversanctuarypublishing.com

We offer personalized service for custom book design and production with worldwide availability through print-on-demand. Specializing in inspirational, spiritual and self-help books, biography, poetry and memoirs.

www.ingramcontent.com/pod-product-compliance
Lightning Source LLC
LaVergne TN
LVHW051830080426
835512LV00018B/2802